Helping Others
on the Journey

Helping Others on the Journey

A guide for those who seek to mentor others to maturity in Christ

Terry Wardle

Sovereign World

Sovereign World Ltd
PO Box 777
Tonbridge
Kent TN11 0ZS
England

ISBN 1 85240 402 7

Cover design by CCD, www.ccdgroup.co.uk
Typeset by CRB Associates, Reepham, Norfolk
Printed in the United States of America

Contents

Dedication

To my dear friend, David Hall
For all the years you have faithfully walked alongside my son.
I will be forever grateful.

Acknowledgements

The central premise of this book is that people need help on the journey of life. One place where I find that principle particularly true is with publishing a book. While I spend a great deal of time alone when writing, there are many people who support the process. They all deserve more recognition than they receive, and the least I can do is offer my deep thanks here. My wife, Cheryl, and family are a constant source of life and joy, and I would not want to walk this journey without them. There are special friends who offer great encouragement and believe in me far more than I believe in myself. I extend special thanks to Anne, John, Peter, Judy, Bob, Fred, and Lee. My administrative assistants, Lynne Lawson and Lori Byron, go way beyond the call of duty and deserve recognition, as does my research assistant Kari White. Tim Pettingale of Sovereign World Publishing is due special thanks for being a constant source of support and for publishing my most recent books.

There is a unique group of men and women who deserve mention because they were the primary source of motivation for developing this resource. In 2002 Ashland Theological Seminary received a generous grant from the Lilly Foundation to support a special program for pastors. During the first phase, eighteen gifted pastors spent a year learning to be spiritual guides for people in pastoral ministry. Each pastor agreed to then help five other pastors journey toward greater effectiveness in life and ministry. I have spent a significant amount of time with these eighteen leaders and have grown to love and respect them dearly. In many ways they have become friends on the journey through life. This resource was written with them in mind.

Brian White	Marc Neal
Chuck Congram	Marilynn Schroeder
David Oliver	Mark Hosler
Fred Miller	Matthew Lewis
Gina Kim	Mike Woods
James Widmer	Nathan Ward
Joseph Stevenson	Stephen Hendry
Kevin Thomas	Neal May
Terry Hofecker	Dale Schaefer

Chapter 1

Life Is a Journey

In 1938, award winning director John Ford went into Monument Valley to film an adaptation of the Ernest Haycox short story, *Stage to Lordsburg*, originally published in *Collier's* magazine. The producer of the film was Walter Wanger, and the cast included then famous stars Clair Trevor, Andy Devine, Louise Platt, John Carradine, Thomas Mitchell and Donald Meek. Ford also took a chance on a relatively unknown actor named John Wayne in the role of the Ringo Kid. The title he ultimately chose for the picture was *Stagecoach*, and as they say, "the rest is history."

Stagecoach is by far my favorite film of all time. It is a wonderful story, set in the nineteenth-century American southwest, centered upon nine people who board a stagecoach in the town of Tonto, bound for Lordsburg, New Mexico. They all have different reasons, good and bad, for wanting to go to Lordsburg.

Dallas is the scarlet woman, chased from Tonto by the upstanding women of that small community who symbolize a heartless form of religious legalism. Dr Jonah Boone is an over-the-hill alcoholic doctor who long ago wore out his usefulness to the townspeople. Samuel Peacock is a traveling whiskey salesman on his way to Lordsburg before returning to his home in Kansas City, Kansas. Lucy Mallory is a southern aristocrat who is on the final leg of her journey west to be reunited with her husband who is stationed at the fort near Lordsburg. Henry Gatewood is the banker of Tonto, who has secretly stolen all the money from the local bank, leaving town on the Lordsburg stage. Hatfield is a bigoted Confederate officer who is trying to hide his past under the guise of a career gambler. Buck is the reluctant stagecoach driver who is nervous about the treacherous journey through hostile Indian country, and Sheriff Curly Wilcox rides shotgun and serves as the self-appointed leader of this band of misfits. Finally, there is the infamous Ringo Kid, who is headed for Lordsburg to avenge the death of his father and brother at the hands of the notorious Plummers.

The journey to Lordsburg is marked by unexpected trials that reveal who these people really are and provide opportunities for personal growth for those who step into the moment willingly. An Indian attack, an unexpected birth, and other unanticipated struggles along the way expose the face of prejudice and greed, evoke moments of undeserved kindness, demand deep personal sacrifice, and present each person with the opportunity to say "yes" to deep change. The interaction between these very different personalities and the struggles they encounter along the way to Lordsburg brings out the courage still present in a washed-out doctor, the softness deep within a hardened prostitute, and the sensitivity and shyness of the notorious Ringo Kid. They each experience a transformation that leaves them all quite different from when they started the journey in Tonto. That is all except for Gatewood, who continually refuses to consider his own depravity, holding to his sinful justification that somehow he deserves the money he has taken from the people who trusted him. In the end, his unwillingness to expose the true motives of his own heart takes Gatewood into a long imprisonment, while the others find in Lordsburg freedom and a new chance at life. *Stagecoach* is far more than a simple western. It is ultimately a story of redemption, a perfect metaphor for life as a journey.

Life Is a Journey

Christians should have no problem conceptualizing life as a journey of transformation. It is a familiar theme throughout

Scripture including the journey of Abraham to the promised land, Moses and the Israelites into the land of Canaan, Jesus and the journey to Jerusalem and Calvary, and Paul and his journey to Rome and eventual martyrdom. In each narrative, as with the fictional journey to Lordsburg, there was a journey over time, a clearly defined destination, unexpected trials and challenges along the way that provided opportunity for personal growth and change, and fellow travelers who were not always in harmony with each other. After all, Abraham had his Lot, Moses his Dathan, and Jesus His Judas. The path each took, the struggles they faced, and the people they encountered were all part of a grand redemptive story.

It does not take much of a creative imagination to see that the journey metaphor is very instructive about life itself. I find this particularly true when trying to help people understand what it means to be a Christian. Many believers are caught in either the *courtroom* or *classroom* models of the Christian life. The first emphasizes that Jesus is the advocate for the condemned, and the second prioritizes the place of sound doctrine as foundational to faith in Christ. Both hold forth important truths related to the Christian life. However, both ultimately fall short as metaphors of faith because they are not comprehensive enough to include the essential transformational dynamic so foundational to following Jesus Christ. The Christian life is far more than being freed from the consequences of sin and/or understanding propositional truth related to Christian beliefs.

The Christian life is a transforming journey, with a clearly defined destination, ongoing challenges that provide opportunities for personal growth, and vital relationships with fellow travelers who do not always seem to like one another. These essential elements of the journey metaphor provide an incredible context for personal transformation, which is in fact the very essence of redemption itself. I believe that these four words: *journey, destination, challenges,* and *fellow travelers,* provide insight into what it means to be a Christian. As people come to understand and embrace the Christian life as a journey, they begin to move forward and grow in very important ways.

Journey

Richard Rohr is a Franciscan priest who founded the Center for Action and Contemplation in Albuquerque, New Mexico. He has authored numerous books and spends a great amount of time lecturing and holding retreats internationally. His book, *Hope Against Darkness*, is a profound challenge to believers, calling the followers of Christ to be agents of change in changing times within a complex world. Rohr chooses to address this theme from the Life of Saint Francis who chose to journey with Christ as a "poor servant" of the broken and lost in society. In this book, Rohr encourages believers to adopt a journey motif for the Christian life. He writes:

> "The Bible seems to always be saying that this journey is indeed a journey, a journey always initiated and con-cluded by God, and a journey of transformation much more than mere education about anything. We would sooner have textbooks, I think. Then the journey would remain a spectator sport, as much religion seems to be. The education model elicits a low level of commitment and investment, even if it keeps people obedient and orthodox. The transformational model risks people know-ing and sharing 'the One Spirit that was given us all to drink' (1 Corinthians 12:13). So sad that we have preferred conformity and group loyalty over real change!"[1]

Real change occurs as Christians respond to the call to journey with Jesus, meeting God in the particulars of day to day life. It is not so important that one knows every detail about the path they will take in life. But what one discovers about oneself and God along the way is critically important to the process of

---

[1]   Rohr, Richard, *Hope Against Darkness: The Transforming Vision of Saint Francis in an Age of Anxiety* (Cincinnati, Ohio: St. Anthony Messenger Press, 2001), p. 12.

transformation and change. In this process of discovery, the pilgrim allows the Spirit of Christ to redeem and recreate him in very deep and important ways. This change demands surrender and willingness, foundational responses to the call of Jesus Christ. Surrender on the journey involves laying down personal agenda and self-interest. Willingness is the prerequisite for picking up the cross of Christ – the losing of one's life so necessary to finding true life, eternal life.

The Christian, over time, traverses all kinds of terrain through all types of weather as he or she moves forward toward the destination set forth for all believers before the foundation of the earth. This destination is very important to everything it means to be Christian. It is not enough to keep moving. The followers of Christ must be moving in a very specific direction. Believers are to be on a journey that takes them ultimately to Jesus Christ and the call to be like Him.

Destination

When my children were young we regularly combined business with pleasure when it came to family vacations. I was often invited to speak at various places across the country and would yearly say "yes" to some event where we could stay on and have a family holiday. This enabled us to combine expenses in a way that made family vacations more afford-able. We all have the best memories from these special journeys and often spend hours reminiscing about wonderful times together.

Whenever someone in my family wants to share memories of a journey, he or she need only mention the destination and the conversation begins. Aaron might begin by asking if we remember the trip to Alberta, when we visited Jasper, Banff and Calgary. My daughter Cara, seems to like to talk about the trips to Florida we took over the years, and Emily, our youngest remembers our vacation in New England, when we journeyed through Vermont, New Hampshire and Maine. In some special way, remembering the destination of a specific journey brings together all the stories that were shaped along the way. The very mention of the specific destination evokes great feelings and the fondest of memories of the time we shared. We all seem to overflow with important life memories shaped on very special journeys together. So it is with the Christian life: destination is a critical part of the journey with Christ.

Just what is the destination of the Christian journey through life? At one level the argument can be made that it is a place, the eternal Kingdom of God, heaven. Jesus assured His followers that He was going there to prepare a place for them and promised to return someday in order to guide believers to their final home (John 14:1–3). The book of Revelation speaks of this special destination, providing a breathtaking word picture of heaven in chapters 20 and 21. It is described as a place of eternal life and light, filled with joyful praise, rest and the fullness of God's healing presence, all made accessible to believers through the sacrifice of Jesus Christ upon Calvary.

The importance of heaven should never be underestimated in the Christian life. It provides great hope to all believers, and comfort to those who have lost loved ones now present with the Lord in glory. There are more than a few of my friends and family members who have passed from this life into the next. And while I miss them, I often find great peace in remembering that they are more alive than I am, rejoicing in heaven with the church triumphant. We would all do well to pay more attention to the promised home that Christ is now preparing for all who believe. It would remind us that our citizenship is truly not of this world.

But having said this, the destination that I believe to be essential to the journey being discussed in this book is not in fact heaven. The Bible seems quite clear that Christians are to be on a journey toward Christ-likeness, a pilgrimage that leads to spiritual maturity and freedom. The progress individuals make on the journey of faith is not measured by how much people know about propositional truth, or how well they behave in front of others, or how diligently they serve within the Christian community. Believers are instead to be focused upon how much they are being changed, through the work of the Holy Spirit, into the likeness of Jesus Christ.

In his second letter to the church at Corinth, Paul wrote:

> *"Now the Lord is the Spirit, and where the Spirit of the Lord is, there is freedom. And we, who with unveiled faces all reflect the Lord's glory, are being transformed into his likeness with ever-increasing glory, which comes from the Lord, who is the Spirit."* (2 Corinthians 3:17–18)

Granted, the entire concept may be difficult to comprehend. Yet there is little question regarding the work the Holy Spirit is seeking to do in believers' lives. He seeks to daily transform Christians into the likeness of Jesus Christ. Ultimately this is the destination of the Christian journey while believers walk upon this earth. Followers of Christ are all called to move toward Christ and His likeness. This truth is not only found in the above passage, but also emphasized in Romans 8:29, Colossians 2:1–9, and Philippians 3:10–14. Though each passage states this truth in its unique way, the theme is the same. Christians are on a journey toward Christ-likeness and must willingly surrender to the Holy Spirit who ministers this deep transforming work. It is change, not knowledge that identifies a person as a follower of Christ. It will not be textbooks that non-believers read to discover the power of the cross. It will be people transformed into the likeness of Christ.

I have written extensively about the call to Christ-likeness in *Outrageous Love, Transforming Power: How the Holy Spirit Shapes you into the likeness of Christ*, published by Sovereign World International. I do not intend to revisit that discussion in detail here. However, I do think it important to at least mention three foundational points related to the journey toward Christ-likeness. First, I am convinced that the nature of Christ is implanted in all believers at the point of conversion. As the Holy Spirit comes to cleanse a person's heart and indwell his or her renewed spirit, He also creates within that individual a new nature that reflects the nature of Jesus. Granted, that new nature is only in seed-like form, needing the nourishing and nurturing work of the Holy Spirit. But it is the nature of Christ and holds the potential for a Christian to mature into His likeness along the journey through life.

Second, there are several identifiable characteristics of Christ that are foundational to this journey to spiritual maturity. The following list is representative of the call to Christ-likeness, qualities that are ready to be nurtured and nourished in every believer's life. Each characteristic listed below was certainly present in Jesus as He walked on earth and are equally important to the call to become mature in Christ for all believers.

- Increasing intimacy with the Father in heaven
- Security in one's identity as a child of God
- Commitment to grow in the context of Christian community
- Transformed character that reflects the character of Jesus
- Brokenness as the context for personal growth
- Ministry that flows from weakness as well as strength
- Walking in the authority of Christ
- Being empowered by the Holy Spirit

These characteristics of Christ-likeness are, in fact, the definition of Christian maturity and as such shape the destination of the Christian journey through life. Simply said, we are to become like Jesus. All of life is to move toward that all important goal.

Third, this personal transformation cannot be achieved by human effort alone. It takes the ministry of the Holy Spirit to bring this level of change to pass. He alone holds the power necessary to change haters into lovers, the greedy into the generous, the insecure into the confident, and the selfish into the self-giving. But having said this, believers dare not think this means that there is no personal involvement in this process of spiritual maturation. Christians must, as previously mentioned, be surrendered and willing. They must understand the call to Christ-likeness and say "yes" to the sanctifying work of the Holy Spirit. Spiritual maturation demands allegiance to Christ and an active willingness to allow the Holy Spirit to accomplish deep, personal transformation. That level of change happens as people respond to Him in the challenges of day-to-day life upon the journey. The destination is now clearly defined, but the events along the way provide the real context for personal transformation.

Struggles and challenges

The journey through life is far from easy. It is filled with challenges and struggles that at times seem to rise from the depths of darkness, hell-bent on destroying all hope and meaning for existence. To say otherwise would take a level of denial that would border on the pathological. Said simply, life can be tough, very tough. Even as you read this, there are people facing trials that seem to assault them at the core of life itself. Loss, sickness, disease, betrayal, poverty, hunger, war and death are ever-present realities in this fallen world. Many people react by adopting an existential fatalism that is best represented by the bumper sticker that reads, "Life is a bitch and then you die."

But Christians do not share this view. At the center of our faith is the conviction that God created life and it was in fact *good* (Genesis 1:31). Life was given as a gift of the Father, full of wonderful possibilities, grounded in unconditional love and filled with meaning and joy. But unfortunately the fall introduced a level of brokenness into the world that has brought great harm to all that God declared to be good. Light has been replaced by a destructive darkness that robs, kills and destroys. But because of Christ, the fall is far from the final word.

Jesus told His followers that He came to bring abundant life to all who believe (John 10:10). Christ was sent by God on a mission of love to redeem this fallen planet. He accomplished this by confronting the forces of evil that set this destruction into motion when they rebelled against the goodness of the Father. Jesus confronted the powers of darkness through acts of love, kindness, healing and deliverance, and then defeated them through His death on Calvary. While, as Jesus said, this world will still present His followers with trouble, He has overcome the world (John 16:33).

The journey through life is still far from easy. But because of Christ it affords great opportunities for personal transformation when Christians respond to challenges and struggles with faith in God's greater purposes. I am not suggesting that God is behind all the trials and suffering that Christians face in life. Not at all. But I do believe that the events that comprise day-to-day existence hold great potential for individual growth. If people respond properly to trials, offering them to God as a vehicle for personal transformation, great changes can and will take place. I have come to call this God's "all things" plan.

Romans 8:28 is a favorite text for Christians. It holds the promise that God works all things together for good for His children. But I believe that Romans 8:29 is essential to understanding what this means in the believer's life. That verse states that God has planned from the very beginning that people would be conformed to the image of Christ. Again, the destination of the life journey is clear. People are to become like Christ. With that in mind, verse 28 takes on new importance. What does God use to work this transformation in people's lives? All things! Every challenge and struggle that Christians face along the journey of life can be used of God to change them into the likeness of Christ. That is, if believers respond properly to these challenges, offering each event to God as a pathway to *"betterness"*, rather than *bitterness*. This is far from easy, given what life brings to people, but with Christ personal transformation can result from even the greatest trials.

Calvin Miller has written a wonderful devotional book that addresses the journey to Christ-likeness. The book is entitled

The Unchained Soul, and includes a thorough examination of truths gleaned from the classic writings of people like Augustine, Madam Guyon, Brother Lawrence, Bernard of Clairvaux and John Bunyon. Miller provides a rich resource that will help any pilgrim move forward toward the destination of spiritual maturity. In the introduction, Miller makes an important statement about the process of personal transformation. He writes:

> "Of this we may be sure: Saints do not spring holy from the forehead of God. They are made, crisis by crisis, need by need. Those who wish to be conformed to his image only make real progress after they discover their own insufficiency."[2]

Christians encounter change crisis by crisis along the journey of life. For many, it is the challenge of great trial and difficulty that exposes the true self, initiating the cry to be forever transformed by the mercy of God's great love.

Frankly, I have spent a considerable amount of time in the ditch as I have journeyed through life. At times I have ended up there because of my own stupidity. At other times I have been the victim of schemes that originated with dark forces. But regardless of the ultimate cause, these crises have provided a context for incredible personal change – and the type of change that occurred was always directly related to my response in the moment of trial. If I became overcome by bitterness and resentment, I ended up looking quite different from Jesus. But, if in the midst of my agony and lament I was able to cry out to God, offering the moment as a pathway to deep change, good things actually resulted from very bad times.

Nowhere has this been more true than when I experienced a deep personal breakdown that ultimately sent me into a

---

2   Miller, Calvin, *The Unchained Soul* (Minneapolis, Minn: Bethany House Publishers, 1998), p. xxi.

psychiatric hospital for extended treatment. The bottom fell out of my world and I ended up deeply depressed and suffering from a debilitating anxiety disorder. I had somehow pressed my face through the thin veil between sanity and insanity and wondered if I would ever again enjoy a peaceful moment in life. But sitting on my hospital bed I remembered the words of Corrie ten Boon. She once commented that the object of great pain could become the source of incredible blessing, if one would offer the trial to God.

With what little faith I had left, I, that day, offered my nightmare to God as a potential opportunity for great change. While the journey had countless tough days ahead, God heard that prayer and used the crisis to change my life as nothing else has before or since. Jesus brought light out of the darkness, initiating a level of intimacy, empowerment and relational growth that has been incredible. My role was simply to be honest about the struggle, entrust it to God's care and surrender to the work He wanted to do in my life. The Father has been faithful and to this day I am reaping the harvest of the simple prayer I made, when I asked God to use my breakdown as part of His "all things" plan for my life.

Once again we see that life is a journey, with Christians called to move forward toward the ultimate destination of spiritual maturity and Christ-likeness. But the path is not easy. It is full of challenges and struggles that hold the potential to either make or break every pilgrim along the way. The difference between victory and defeat rests with the Christian's response to each trial. When surrendered and willing, God will use these events to bring a level of change that will last throughout eternity. The Christian will become more like Jesus. But if the response is one of resentment, bitterness and rebellion, the change will only lead to bondage and greater brokenness. One final fact of the journey must be discussed. There are others who move along the path, fellow pilgrims through life. How the believer responds to them is an important part of personal growth and transformation.

Fellow travelers

I think one of the main reasons I like the film *Stagecoach* is because it is not about the classic western hero who single-handedly saves the day. It is a story about the interrelationship of very different people joined by fate on a difficult journey, facing incredible challenges that threaten their very lives. The fact that it takes place in the American west is really only a minor part of the story. It is a tale that could have been set in any place, at any time in history. *Stagecoach* is a powerful metaphor for life itself, which very much involves people being thrown together on a potentially life-changing journey through time.

As I reflect upon my life I am quite taken by the cast of characters who comprise this chapter of my own story. There are the members of my family who have always played a critical role in my life. Added to that are special friends who, through thick and thin, seem to have my wellbeing always in mind. I have casual friends and colleagues with me on the journey. Some of these people seem to view me positively, in spite of my own particular idiosyncrasies. Others find me more than a little hard to take, which in truth I can understand. I can at times be difficult to handle. To be honest, I pretty much share the same opinion about several of them. That's life.

But what is important to remember is that my response to the people I am with on this journey through life is very important, to me and to them. It is critical that we grow to increasingly reveal our true selves. Why? Because there is far too much at risk to pretend to be something we are not. Lives are often in the balance and pretense does not make for an environment conducive to deep personal transformation. Change happens as fellow pilgrims openly face personal inadequacy and insufficiency in light of the challenges life affords.

There is, frankly, far too much pretending going on in the church today. People, including leaders, seem committed to relating to one another out of a carefully constructed false self.

True attitudes, feelings, weaknesses and struggles are hidden away from public view. Why? Because of a great fear that if others really knew them, rejection and disqualification would result. And so people hide, pretend, and behave as well as possible. But deep change never happens because transformation demands a level of vulnerability. People who pretend end up along the side of the path, deeply wounded and disabled because they did not get the support they really needed along the way. Granted, such openness can be discomforting, but change demands the surrender of the false self, so that fellow pilgrims can grow to offer honest support through the journey we call life.

Consider the life of Jesus. He surrounded Himself with a community of fellow pilgrims who were certainly not easy to take. He had two brothers with anger problems, a couple of insurrectionists, a Roman collaborator, a tough-talking fisherman, a follower who was a bit of a skeptic and a bright Judean who ultimately disagreed with Christ and betrayed Him. But they walked together for three years through some very difficult challenges. And in the end, they were, except for the bright Judean, transformed people. They allowed the character of Christ to confront their own biases and struggles, ultimately laying down their lives to tell the story of His life. Along the way they began to look more and more like Jesus, which is the ultimate purpose of life itself. In the end, they each made it to their own "Lordsburg", deeply changed human beings because of the journey they made together.

The Call to Help Others Along the Way

I now finally come to the purpose for this book. Christians need help as they make the journey through life. It is easy to get lost and disoriented along the way, as many have done throughout history. Without the proper help, Christians can make wrong turns that lead to great disaster. They can fail to properly anticipate the terrain and be significantly hurt along the path. As with all journeys, the weather is a factor and when the Christian enters a changing season unprepared, he or she can experience a debilitating level of personal discomfort. And, like it or not, there are dark places along the way where robbers and thieves wait to steal, kill and destroy. The journey toward Christ-likeness holds many challenges. It is best if Christians make this journey together and it is essential that there be a guide who has traveled the path long enough to help others move forward toward the Lord.

This book is designed as a resource for spiritual guides, men and women who feel called and empowered of the Lord to help others journey toward Christ-likeness. The chapters that follow each address some essential aspect of being a spiritual guide. Chapter 2 focuses upon the privilege and responsibility that exists when serving others in this special ministry. Special attention is given to the essential values and virtues that must be present within the person who says "yes" to this type of ministry. Chapter 3 in turn talks about the necessary characteristics of those who want to be helped along the journey, and the commitments that are essential to a healthy relationship between spiritual guide and pilgrim. In chapter 4 there is an important discussion regarding the resources that are fundamental to this journey, namely the ministry of the Holy Spirit, Scripture, time and the gift of discernment.

Chapter 5 focuses upon the context that best serves spiritual guidance, with specific discussion of various formats available for this type of direction. In chapter 6 the "all things" plan of God will be developed, followed by specific principles of spiritual guidance that best position Christians for deep change and personal growth. The tools and exercises of spiritual guidance will be treated in chapter 7, followed in chapter 8 with a discussion of the different seasons of growth that people encounter along the way toward Christ-likeness.

As mentioned previously, there are enemies along the way. Chapter 9 presents a balanced, biblical and highly practical view of spiritual warfare as it relates to the ministry of spiritual guidance. The book concludes with a discussion of the joy that results from serving fellow believers in this incredible ministry.

In this often confusing and complex age, the need for guidance and direction along life's path is critical. People need help responding to the challenges of life in ways that enhance personal growth and spiritual maturity. They need to understand that life is a journey, with a clear view to the destination that is Christ Himself. People also need help relating to life events in ways that enhance growth, all the while appreciating the relationships so essential to the journey. Saying "yes" to the unique ministry of spiritual guide, while most certainly humbling, is a wonderful opportunity to serve Christ while serving others. And in the end, great transformation becomes possible, not only for those being guided, but for those who embrace this special call.

Chapter 2

Becoming a Spiritual Guide

The Lord Christ has graciously chosen to lay His hand upon me for the ministry of spiritual guidance. Granted, it is not my primary calling. I spend most of my time as a seminary professor, teaching men and women who are preparing to enter vocational Christian service. But almost every day, in both planned and spontaneous ways, I find myself helping a brother or sister in Christ move forward on the journey of life. Whether sitting together in my office, enjoying a walk through the surrounding neighborhood, speaking on the telephone, or sharing thoughts over email, I am privileged to help very precious people respond to life in ways that invite personal change. It is a wonderful experience.

John Kent is director for training at Adventists Frontier Mission. His wife Belinda is a dear child of God who has a hunger for Christ that is exciting to watch. Long ago they gave their lives to the cause of Christ. They are special people who are deeply dedicated to global evangelism. In the 1990s, John and Belinda went to New Guinea as missionaries to unreached people. Neither had the benefit of college or seminary education when they went to New Guinea. But they, along with their small children, traveled into a primitive culture for the cause of Christ. There they set up a home, established a medical center and went on to start a church. God profoundly blessed their ministry, but the toll upon their personal lives was great.

I met John and Belinda through a mutual friend who brought them for a time of healing prayer. Years of ministry had taken a toll upon them and the Kents needed to find the path to refreshing in Christ. As we spent time together the Lord poured out His goodness upon their lives and ushered them into a special season of renewal and refreshing. Recently, the Kents asked me if I would help them move forward on their journey toward Christ. I was overwhelmed with the awesome privilege and responsibility that was attached to their request. Such wonderful people, asking me to help them along the way. Amazing. But the witness of the Spirit confirmed that the Lord would have me serve His children in this way. I do it, not because I feel worthy, but because I know I am called. It is not my wisdom and brilliance that impacts the process, but His Holy Spirit, who anoints His chosen vessel with insight and inspiration that comes from beyond myself. By His great mercy the Lord even uses the trials and challenges of my past to impact their present journey. In my weakness He becomes strong and in my insufficiency He is always more than enough to bring lasting change in people's lives.

I also serve as a spiritual guide because I have been so helped by people who cared enough to direct me along the path. I would never have grown as a Christian if it had not been for the guidance I received from very special people who willingly walked with me, stayed with me when I hesitated, supported me when I stumbled, cared for me when I was hurt along the way, prayed for me when I doubted, and consistently pointed me to Jesus. These people are saints and the love and appreciation I feel for them will last into and throughout eternity.

Gene Evans is now part of the church triumphant, passing into the Lord's presence in 2003. I will never be able to adequately describe the impact this dear man had upon my spiritual journey. He spent his life serving as a missionary, first in China and then Vietnam. Gene was unquestionably the most accepting and affirming man I have even known. His love and patience with me, through some very difficult times was life changing. He invested in me when there was really no reason for him to do so. Yet he gave with an enthusiasm and generosity that made me feel special. Frankly, everyone who encountered Gene felt that way. It was his gift to us all. He and he alone was responsible for my moving from pastoral to seminary ministry, able in one anointed conversation to change the direction of my ministry and ultimately my life.

Grandma Sanders also holds a unique place in my heart. Her husband Bill was my first little league baseball coach and she my first spiritual guide. Grandma Sanders was a saintly African-American woman who embraced me as her spiritual son. She regularly prayed for me, often gave me words of direction and encouragement, and never failed to remind me that life was all about Jesus. Several years ago, while lying ill with pancreatic cancer, she asked to see me once again. I had traveled from California to Pennsylvania in time to speak with her before her passing. Grandma Sanders shared two words that she believed were important for me. They were so profound that I cannot share them here, but hold them as gifts deep within my heart. Grandma Sanders pointed the way for me many times and whatever I have become in life is in part a result of her faithful guidance in service to Christ. Her name may not be well known among the living, but I am sure that all heaven knows the story of her faithful journey through life with Jesus.

My spiritual guides include saints of the past who left written guidance for those who would follow in future generations. I have been profoundly shaped by the seventeenth-century quietists like Francois Fenelon and Madam Guyon. Reading the works of eighteenth-century Christians like Jonathan Edwards, George Whitefield, John Wesley and Jean-Pierre de Caussald continue to help me navigate difficult times as little else can. Finney, Moody, Simpson and Spurgeon, nineteenth-century spiritual giants, are a rich resource of spiritual direction that have proven to be invaluable to me. More recently, I have been greatly helped by the writings of contemporaries like Henri Nouwen, LeAnne Payne, David Watson, Richard Foster, Calvin Miller, Dallas Willard, and Richard Rohr. I am well aware that none of the people I have mentioned know who I am. But they know the journey toward Christ-likeness and their ministries of spiritual guidance have profoundly impacted countless lives, not the least of which is mine.

Being a spiritual guide is an important ministry, particularly in this postmodern age marked by excess, loneliness, confusion and irrelevancy. Helping people along life's journey, be it a single individual or small group of fellow pilgrims, is an indescribable privilege that holds incredible potential and possibilities for lasting change. Many who want to enter vocational Christian service do not understand the value of this often hidden, quiet ministry. Christians can easily fall prey to the allure of the large, public ministries that provide recognition and a certain degree of broad acclaim.

Anyone who has spent time serving Christ knows that the time invested in the few brings forth far more change than that which is given to larger, more public ministries. While I am grateful for the opportunity to speak to large crowds of people, I am aware that the lasting impact of such events is limited. But the investments I make with one, two, or three people, specifically given for spiritual guidance, bears fruit that lasts. There I see change occur, which is certainly the purpose of a life spent in service to Christ. Being a spiritual guide is a high calling and as Paul suggested in 1 Timothy 3:1, anyone who sets his or her heart to it aspires to a noble task.

What Does it Mean to Be a Spiritual Guide?

The ministry of guiding another person on the journey to Christ-likeness has been written about throughout the centuries, identified by different, yet related titles. Early mystics called people who served others in this way *spiritual fathers* and *mothers*, emphasizing the role of nurturer and parent in spiritual development. During the days of Saint

John of the Cross and Teresa of Avila it was known as *spiritual direction* and those who served were called *spiritual directors*. This designation seemed to emphasize the importance of submission and authority necessary to spiritual growth. More recently the term *spiritual mentor* has become popular, with particular emphasis upon the more practical aspects of spiritual development. There are also those who speak of *spiritual friends* or *spiritual companions* who provide encouragement and direction along the path to Christ. These terms each highlight the relational component essential to spiritual growth, often prioritizing mutuality and peer support.

Each of the previous terms is instructive to the role of spiritual guidance, rightly prioritizing one or more of the necessary dynamics intrinsic to this ministry. But, for the purpose of this discussion, I am choosing to use the term *spiritual guide* since it fits best with the journey motif. It also prioritizes what I believe to be essential to this ministry, pointing the way to Jesus and Christ-likeness. However, many of the nuances of the designations listed earlier are intrinsic to the concept. Being a spiritual guide certainly involves nurture, submission, authority, spiritual friendship, mutuality and mentoring opportunities. But being a spiritual guide is always, first and foremost, about movement toward Christ and His likeness. Everything that the spiritual guide does along the way is intended to serve this ultimate purpose.

Simply stated, I define being a spiritual guide as the process of helping others respond to the journey of life in ways that invite personal transformation into the image of Jesus Christ. It may be helpful to this discussion to break out several of the components of this definition for further explanation.

Being a spiritual guide is a process ... Spiritual guidance often happens in moments of time, but it also occurs over extended seasons in a person's life. Like any journey, movement occurs one step at a time, covering different kinds of terrain, in the face of unique challenges and struggles. The spiritual guide understands this process and commits to journey with others, not simply stand at one spot and point the way. The length of this commitment may vary due to circumstance and need. But the spiritual guide is well aware that life is a journey and personal transformation far more of a process than a one-time event.

Being a spiritual guide is a process *of helping others* ... The spiritual guide does not seek to exercise control over another person, nor does he want the pilgrim to become dependent for personal growth and maturity. The spiritual guide does not dictate or lord it over another person. Instead the spiritual guide seeks to influence personal growth and mature responsibility. Healthy guidance always leads people to increasing well-being and freedom, not co-dependent relationships between guide and follower. Certainly helping demands involvement, care, and great attention to the life of the Christian being served. But helping also has its limits, shaped by the kind of love that invites deep personal change.

Being a spiritual guide is the process of helping others *respond to the journey of life in ways that invite personal transformation* ... As discussed in the previous chapter, life is full of struggles and challenges. Many people react to such difficulties in ways that ultimately invite greater destruction and harm. The spiritual guide seeks to help others respond to life in ways that will position them for change. Surrender and willingness are essential to this response, attitudes that are not so easy to have when times are trying. Through encouragement and anointed guidance, the spiritual guide helps Christians embrace the "all things plan" of God that invites His transforming presence.

Being a spiritual guide is the process of helping others respond to the journey of life in ways that invite personal transformation *into the image of Christ*. Once again we return to the ultimate destination of life's journey. As Henri Nouwen once wrote, "the Gospel simply stated is: become like Jesus." The journey to Christ is in fact the very meaning of life. The healthy spiritual guide knows that and remains committed to the centrality of Christ. There can be no compromise on this point. The spiritual guide serves a purpose far greater than helping individuals become better persons or spiritual in some general sense. He or she is called to help people say "yes" to the transformation that makes them changed persons who increasingly reflect the glory of Christ. While such a notion may appear to be narrow in an age of religious pluralism, it remains the center toward which all of life is intended to move. The spiritual guide must be faithful to this central truth.

Father Thomas Green wrote that a spiritual guide is ultimately "a wise companion on the journey of life," who encourages others to remain open to the experience of life, open to themselves, and ultimately open to what God is doing in their lives.[3] The person who serves others in this way will witness the most amazing transformation possible in people's lives. He will watch as people begin to look more and more like Jesus, the Christ. Can there be a more important calling than this? Is there any greater privilege? Could there be a more serious responsibility?

What Characteristics Are Essential to Being a Spiritual Guide?

I am continually struck by the tenderness Jesus showed to the broken as He walked this earth. He treated the weak with incredible love and extended an acceptance to the sinner that changed their lives. At the same time Jesus called them beyond their sin to a holy life. Jesus spent time with tax collectors who were robbing their own people, and in response they became generous children of the Kingdom, like Zacchaeus (Luke 19:1–9). Jesus refused to condemn an adulterous woman even when the law gave room to take her life for her actions (John 8:1–11). Jesus embraced the outcasts of society and promised them a special place in heaven, providing through His death a righteousness that they could never earn or deserve

---

[3]   Green, Thomas, *The Friend of the Bridegroom* (Notre Dame, Indiana: Ave Maria Press, 1999), p. 27.

(Luke 23:43). I cannot adequately describe the comfort and hope that floods my soul when I contemplate the wondrous love of Jesus. It is truly a kindness from God that leads to repentance (Romans 2:4).

It is also quite amazing to consider how often Jesus gave power and authority to very imperfect people. The disciples are certainly important examples of this. There are more than a few occasions in the gospels when they clearly did not get what Jesus was all about. James and John wanted to call down fire upon the Samaritans rather than extend love (Luke 9:51–55). Peter not only tried to keep Jesus from the journey to Calvary (Matthew 16:21–28), but denied Him when Jesus needed him most (Matthew 26:69–75). His followers slept as Jesus agonized in Gethsemane (Matthew 26:36–46), fled when He was arrested (Mark 14:43–52), and at least one, Thomas, doubted the resurrection itself (John 20:24–30).

At the very end, as Jesus was preparing to ascend into glory, the disciples still thought Christ was going to establish a political kingdom in Jerusalem (Acts 1:6). And yet, in spite of all these weaknesses, Jesus commissioned the disciples to carry forward the gospel and establish His church! Granted, He did not leave them alone in this task, empowering each with the baptism of the Holy Spirit (Acts 2:1). I am convinced that Jesus called them because He knew they where thoroughly committed to Him and would in the end give their very lives for the gospel. Jesus saw beyond the brokenness to the incredible potential they held, and in the end they revolutionized the world. Once again, this brings great hope to me, knowing that the call of Christ upon my life is not based upon what I am now, but what I can become in Him.

It is equally important to consider how Jesus treated the appointed spiritual guides of his day, Pharisees, Sadducees and Priests. Rather than tender and patient, Jesus was often harsh and condemning. He openly called them blind guides, whitewashed tombs and a brood of vipers. Jesus was intolerant of their self-righteous pomposity, openly pulling back the veil of their pretense and pride to expose deep spiritual barrenness. The gospel narratives reveal that Jesus was critical of the religious leaders at two points, character and values. When Jesus called them whitewashed tombs He was saying that regardless of position, title, office or authority, they were small people absent of godly character. He saw their greed, pride and selfishness for what it was and refused to be silent about it. Serving as a spiritual guide absent of character was, for Jesus, unacceptable.

The Lord also rejected the values of the spiritual leaders of His day. They were caught up with appearance, religious and political power, and self-importance. They valued long robes, important titles, special privilege and public recognition. Generally speaking, these religious guides cared little about the people they were called to serve. Jesus knew that and openly criticized them for doing far more harm than good in people's lives. The people were precious to Christ and He would not silently sit by and watch as self-possessed hypocrites led them to greater pain rather than freedom and abundant life.

Anyone who feels called to serve as a spiritual guide must carefully consider this discussion. On the one hand, the actions of Jesus toward the broken and insufficient should bring great hope and comfort. He is a tender Savior who shows incredible patience and encouragement to men and women who want to respond to the call to service, while recognizing their own limitations. If they are surrendered and willing, such followers can grow to effectively serve as guides along the journey of life. On the other hand, the spiritual guide must never forget that Jesus cares deeply for those who need help along the way. Serving as a spiritual guide is a high calling that demands character qualities that reflect Christ and values that are consistent with the Kingdom of light and life. It is important that some time be spent looking at those two critical issues which are so foundational to this particular ministry.

The Character of the Spiritual Guide

I asked students in a doctoral class on spiritual direction to identify what they believed to be the most important character qualities of a spiritual guide. Generally speaking we all agreed that it would be important that this person be an individual who was not a new believer, with clear evidence of spiritual maturity. That should be true of anyone serving Christ with primary leadership responsibilities. But when it came to being a spiritual guide, we agreed rather quickly that the following characteristics were indispensable to this particular ministry:

- *humility*
- *love*
- *honesty*
- *patience*
- *sensitivity*
- *trustworthiness.*

The students recognized that some of these characteristics might be more developed than others, but all must be present and maturing in the life of the spiritual guide.

Humility

In the introduction to Margaret Guenther's book, *Holy Listening: The Art of Spiritual Direction*, Alan Jones commented that a spiritual guide needed to be "earthy." That is in fact the core of what true humility is all about. It is the deep personal conviction that we are all created from the dust of the earth and to that dust we will return. The effective spiritual guide knows this and fully recognizes the true potential of his shortcomings and weaknesses. The spiritual guide is unpretentious about his failures and modest about his gifts and abilities. The humble spiritual guide is not judgmental about a person's failings, because she readily admits that there is not a sin another has ever committed that she is not capable of under the same conditions. Humility keeps the spiritual guide focused upon Christ and dependent upon the Holy Spirit as they serve others along the journey. The person being served will always sense that the humble spiritual guide is far more attentive to what the Lord is saying rather than enamored by their own voice.

Love

Scripture is crystal clear about the fact that love is the currency of the Kingdom of God. There is no greater power and there will never be a more lasting virtue (1 Corinthians 13:13). Jesus told His disciples that the love they showed toward one another was the greatest evidence that they belonged to Him (John 13:33–34). The effective spiritual guide is a person who has been captured by the power of God's unconditional love, turning to lavish upon others what the Father has so freely poured out upon him. Paul's description of love in 1 Corinthians chapter 13 is unparalleled in all of literature. That is the love that motivates the effective spiritual guide to serve others along the way. What person on the journey of life does not need this type of love? Who would not be forever changed when touched by this love? Is there any power that invites personal transformation like the love Paul describes? The effective spiritual guide is a servant of love and interested in nothing less for God's people.

Honesty

In the letter to the Church of Ephesus, Paul wrote that growing toward Christ-likeness demands that believers speak the truth to one another in love (Ephesians 4:15). Love and truth are a rare commodity today and yet so essential to spiritual growth. Many people try to love without speaking the truth, which ends up being little more that shallow sentimentality. Others, priding themselves in being frank and forthright, say things in ways that do far more damage than good, actually impeding an individual's progress toward Christ rather than enhancing it. The effective spiritual guide seeks to combine love and truth in a way that produces healthy and helpful honesty. The effective spiritual guide generally sees far more than they say, sharing only those thoughts that are timely to the moment and an individual's progress toward Christ. And what is said is enfolded in an envelope of love that helps a person receive the insight more willingly and openly.

Patience

In a society that feels that instant gratification is not soon enough, the concept of patience seems archaic. But the effective spiritual guide knows that change is a process that takes place over time. There may be instant cash, but there will never be instant Christ-likeness. Spiritual development takes a lifetime of movement in the same direction. Like the farmer who sows seeds in the ground, allowing them to grow secretly and out of sight, the spiritual guide invests in the spiritual growth of others without demanding immediate change or results. The spiritual guide is also aware that people do not always make the best response to life's challenges the first, second, or even third time. The spiritual guide trusts and celebrates the process of spiritual development as much as the fruit; they exercise patient service and watchfulness over those under their care, to the glory of Jesus Christ.

Sensitivity (compassion)

Individuals in western societies today seem to have become anesthetized to the pain that is experienced by most people in the world. They are able to watch the horror of world events without touching the deep emotion that would normally arise within a healthy human being. People have become numb and insensitive. The effective spiritual guide does not share that disease. He is able to empathize with those in deep hurt and approach guidance with sensitivity and care. Helping people through the challenges of life demands that spiritual guides show compassion for the hardships that people experience. There are genuine Christians who desire to grow in Christ, but are at important levels debilitated by the wounds they have experienced in life. The effective spiritual guide understands this and is able to move people forward at a pace that enhances the healing process. The spiritual guide is committed to doing this without pronouncing judgment or shame, knowing well that God can bring light even out of the darkest moments in life.

Trustworthiness

The spiritual guide is certainly a trustworthy Christian who understands that people need to feel safe with the person who is guiding them along life's way. In most cases it will take time before people trust the spiritual guide with their most sensitive issues. But from the very beginning of the relationship the pilgrims will be watching the guide to see if he is worthy of trust. They will want to see if the spiritual guide can keep a confidence or not. Violate this and the relationship may be forever compromised. Individuals will also watch to discover how dependable the spiritual guide is, particularly when it matters most along the journey. And of course, those being served in spiritual guidance will evaluate the level of skill and effectiveness the spiritual guide has. All this will determine the degree to which a people are willing to embrace a spiritual guide on the journey toward Christ-likeness. Trustworthiness is a non-negotiable.

Character matters in spiritual guidance. The effective spiritual guide knows this and allows the Spirit of Christ to continually shape his deep inner life to reflect the Lord's nature. As with all things in spiritual development, the standard is movement toward Jesus far more than perfection. On this side of the Kingdom perfection is out of reach. But every believer has the potential to keep changing under the touch of God's good Spirit. The effective spiritual guide positions himself for that work day by day, and then moves forward to help brothers and sisters struggling along the way.

The Values of the Spiritual Guide

It is critical that, before an individual follows another along the path to Christ, they take time to find out what is truly important to that spiritual guide. Frankly, that happens more by watching what a person does than listening to what he says. Most Christians today can recite at least the fundamental values of the Christian life. The questions is, "Do they live by these values?" Certain core values are indispensable to serving as a spiritual guide and must receive a level of personal investment that produces the spiritual capital essential to this particular task. Personally, I would want a spiritual guide to hold these six values as non-negotiable commitments in life:

- *the pursuit of God*
- *personal well-being*
- *commitment to Christian community*
- *failure*
- *wounded healer ministry*
- *the anointing of the Holy Spirit.*

The pursuit of God

The effective spiritual guide has a passion for God that translates into considerable time in His presence. Many Christian servants today lack sufficient spiritual capital for ministry because they fail to spend time with the Lord. It is just that simple. Ask them if it is important and the answer is most often, "yes." But then begin to ask about the how, what, when, where, and how much of that commitment, and many have little to say. They are busy investing in the *doing* of ministry, all the while neglecting the bread of life that satisfies the deepest hunger of the human heart. The spiritual guide who effectively serves others spends time in the presence of the Lord. It is life to them, satisfying as nothing else. The disciplines of prayer, worship, Word and contemplation are a source of strength, and time is regularly set aside as sacred space meant only for the whispers of God. Guiding another along the path of life demands a level of spiritual vitality that is developed through time with the Lord. For the spiritual guide, personal spirituality matters!

Personal well-being

Being gifted does not necessarily mean that a Christian is also healthy. I found this out the hard way. My gifting far outdistanced my maturity in my early ministry, which eventually ended in a devastating breakdown. The spiritual guide is to be a person who is willing to confront their own dysfunctional behaviors and get the help necessary for personal freedom. Behaviors like people-pleasing, performance addictions, controlling attitudes, manipulation and levels of codependency are destructive. They have no place in Christian ministry. They hurt not only the person who has the dysfunctions, but those who are served by people trapped in them. The spiritual guide is willing to make the inward journey toward personal well-being, knowing that to do less would be to dishonor Christ and the people being served. The journey to wholeness is not without a certain degree of pain. But when addressed before the Lord it is the pain that leads to new life, not death. The effective spiritual guide makes that journey, for God, for others, and ultimately for himself.

Commitment to Christian community

It should be clear by now, particularly from the example and teachings of Christ, that this journey through life is a corporate event. Jesus never intended that there be "Lone Ranger Christians" who forge ahead alone. The call to Christ is unquestionably the call to community. Admittedly, that is not always easy. There are times when it is not fun to walk along the path with people who seem to rub you in the wrong way. But in the economy of God, they are probably rubbing off something that God wants to eliminate from your life. The spiritual guide understands the value of community and makes deep, practical commitments to other believers. He seeks accountability, spends time learning and growing with other Christians, and values the insight and direction that comes from other pilgrims moving toward Christ. A spiritual guide who ministers alone is, in truth, dangerous, open to imbalance and eccentricity. But the guide who stays deeply connected to other believers is positioned to make a great difference in countless lives.

Failure

I am sure that many will question my including failure as a necessary core value for serving as a spiritual guide. But I believe it wholeheartedly and will not easily move from that commitment. I have trouble trusting someone who has not spent at least some time in the ditch. Personally, I have learned far more from my mistakes than from successes, and I am thoroughly convinced that is true of most effective leaders. Individuals who suggest that they have never failed are, as far as I am concerned, either not telling the truth or fairly inexperienced in life. Either way, they should not be followed far along the journey. The effective spiritual guide has scars which serve as constant reminders of God's grace and mercy. He has received comfort from the Lord in tough times and is now able to extend the same to others.

Wounded healer ministry

This core value is in truth a further development of the previous one. I have been literally amazed at how many people turn to me for help since I experienced a personal breakdown. Only in an upside-down kingdom would a trip to a psychiatric hospital actually increase the respect that people have for a person's ministry. I have found that vulnerability and honesty about my own journey helps people embrace their own struggles along the way. I approach serving others from the position of a person still being healed by Christ from deep wounds. And then, from those very places of pain, I am able to point others to the wonder of His love and healing power. The promise that the "object of great pain can become the source of great blessings" has become true, all to the glory of Christ. The effective spiritual guide is and will always be a wounded healer, being changed by Christ as he positions others for the very same miracle.

The anointing of the Holy Spirit

What does it take to be an effective spiritual guide? Most importantly it demands that a person is gifted by the Holy Spirit and spiritually empowered to help others along the journey. There are skills and tools that a person can learn to use in the ministry of spiritual guidance. There are also classes that can be taken that would equip people and books that can be read to build and improve competency. But all that pales in comparison to the importance of the Spirit's anointing upon the spiritual guide. An educational model would demand a degree. A bureaucratic model would insist upon the proper office and authority. But Jesus once said that *"the Spirit gives life; the flesh counts for nothing"* (John 6:63). The words that help people on the journey toward Christ-likeness must be empowered by the Holy Spirit. The effective spiritual guide takes the admonition of Paul seriously, seeking to *"be filled with the Spirit"* over and over again (Ephesians 5:18).

Serving as a spiritual guide is a great privilege and an incredible responsibility. Allowing the Lord to develop godly character and Kingdom values is essential to the ministry of helping others move toward the Lord and personal trans-formation. Through the power of the Holy Spirit, men and women can be effective in this ministry, even in the face of personal weakness and insufficiency. That is the nature of God's grace and the power of the cross of Christ. Now, it is time to turn the discussion to those seeking to be led, which presents an entirely different set of challenges.

Chapter 3

Those Who Follow

Playing "follow the leader" as a child is a whole lot easier than leading people along the journey of life. For one thing, "follow the leader" is a game, life is not. For another, children play "follow the leader" for laughs, but in real life people are not always having a great deal of fun along the way. Consider Moses. He was a spiritual guide and more often than not his followers seemed to want his head on a stick. They second-guessed him all along the way, grumbling and rebelling for forty years, complaining about every challenge that sprang up before them. But God called him to serve as their leader and he stayed at his post until the Lord took him home to glory.

The people of Israel were often unreasonable and demanding, and on numerous occasions proved the adage that "sheep" are not all that bright.

If a person were to ask most pastors what it is like to lead a flock of God's people he would quickly discover that it is a demanding vocation. Personal experience has taught me that God's "sheep" can be vicious. I spent more than my share of time recovering from unexpected "sheep bites" as I tried to pastor the Lord's little flock to better grazing. I wish I had been instructed better about this reality, rather than approaching the ministry with the illusion that being a spiritual guide to a congregation would be all still waters and green pastures. There are challenges to being a spiritual guide over a group of people that are quite demanding, including stubbornness, small thinking, spiritual immaturity and willful disobedience. There are also regular assaults from wolves in sheep's clothing, bent on bringing harm to the people of God. That is certainly not true of everyone in a local church, but is present enough to make things very interesting. Just for the record, there are several people who would share some of these same thoughts relative to trying to help me along the way!

I point to this reality for two important reasons. First, there must be no illusions about guiding others toward Christlikeness. There will be difficulties. The evil one wants to lure people backward, not forward along the path toward Christ. The way is tough, the challenges great and the people being served are not always all that cooperative. Which moves me directly to the second point. The best and most effective spiritual guidance happens with a small group of people, even to the level of one to one, than it does with a larger group. It should not be assumed that pastoring a local congregation affords the best context and opportunity to provide spiritual guidance. This is simply not true. The most productive spiritual guidance will happen as the spiritual guide selectively invests in specific people who are committed to the journey toward Christ. It is important that a spiritual guide exercises great care when determining who to help, for some people are far more ready and eager to move along the path than others.

Consider Jesus and the selection of the twelve disciples. He did not solicit followers by simply making a general announcement and then committing to invest in anyone and everyone who responded. The Lord took great care to prayerfully determine who to invite into relationship with Him. The Bible says that Jesus went up on a mountain to pray and then He called to Himself those He wanted (Mark 3:13). That does not mean that Christ was not concerned about the spiritual wellbeing of the crowds who gathered to hear Him preach. He served them also, but made His deepest investment of spiritual guidance in those few whom He believed were best prepared for that ministry at that time.

It is a fact of life that not all people are at the same place at the same time. When it comes to spiritual guidance, some people are open and ready while others are not. In most cases, the day will arrive when those who may have been resistant will be more prepared to receive direction. The wise spiritual director knows this and invests time where it has the potential to do the most good. This may sound harsh and insensitive to some, but it is the truth just the same. Serving as a spiritual guide is a challenge in even the best of circumstances. Prayerfully selecting the right person or persons to lead along the way is simply a matter of good and faithful stewardship.

I spend a considerable amount of time serving as a spiritual guide, particularly with people who have experienced deep personal loss and wounding. As a rule, because of time limitations and the leading of the Lord, I only invest long term in those people who are committed to ultimately turn and serve in the role of spiritual guide for others. Immediately that narrows the field of possibilities for me. It also, in the end, broadens the impact of my ministry.

Generally speaking, there are two ways in which people come to me for help. First, there are those who make a personal contact and ask for help. They are motivated and willing to do most anything because of the level of pain and discomfort they are experiencing. Second, there are those who are sent to me by churches, denominational agencies, and various missionary groups. Usually these people have acted in ways that have hurt others and they are being required to receive spiritual guidance as a requisite for continuing in ministry. In both cases I must spend time in prayer to determine whom to serve. Time will not allow me to minister to everyone in an effective way, so choices must be made and I try to say "yes" to each person the Lord identifies. However, I realize this truth: those who come by their own choice will make far more progress than those who are sent by someone else. The first group comes motivated by a deep sense of personal need. The second group invariably is resistant and resentful of the process.

It should not be difficult to see that one group of people will, as a rule, make better progress than the other. Obviously the Holy Spirit holds the power to transform anyone He chooses. But experience has taught me that God does not intrude into a life and simply fix matters. He responds to the invitation of surrender and willingness extended by the person seeking deep personal change. People genuinely open to help along the journey are best positioned for change and the spiritual guide should invest most deeply with them. Obviously this recommendation must be made with complete deference to the will of the Holy Spirit. But with that said, prayerful selection regarding whom to help, must be made by the spiritual guide.

In 1999 the senior pastor of a large, mid-western congregation asked if I would spend time helping his associate pastor work through some personal issues. There was tension on the church staff caused by this individual and something had to be done. After seeking the Lord's guidance I agreed to see this pastor. At our very first meeting he let me know that he did not want to be there, felt that he was being unjustly persecuted by the church staff, and did not feel that he had a problem. They did. I met a couple times with him, allowed him the opportunity to vent and offered some practical advice on getting along with others. But it was clear to me that this was as far as things were going to progress. I ended the sessions.

Three-and-one-half years later the associate pastor contacted me. He was hurting deeply and about to give up on pastoral ministry. He asked for help, assuring me that he would do whatever it took to move through this difficult time. We began to meet and it was evident that the Lord was doing a great work in this man's life. There was certainly pain, tears, and a great deal of hard work. But the Holy Spirit was changing him and it was a joy to watch what was happening in his life.

This pastor had become open to himself, open to God, and open to the process. That in turn opened a highway before him that continues to lead him to deep change and significant spiritual growth. The shift in attitude from resistance to willingness and from resentment to relinquishment, made all the difference in the world. When he first came, he was not willing and the time was not right. But when he returned his heart was set to encounter the God who transforms lives. That is when I was best able to serve him and as such truly serve the Lord.

The spiritual guide must be willing to use wisdom and discernment when determining who to help. There is absolutely nothing wrong with this approach to providing spiritual guidance. It is important to remember the principle of ministry that Jesus shared when asked by the Pharisees why He did the things He did. Jesus simply stated that He did what He saw the Father doing (John 5:19). Or, in other words, He served as instructed. Jesus did not heal every sick person, raise all the dead to life, nor turn water into wine at every Judean wedding. While many were touched by His miraculous power, many were not. He acted when and where He felt led and placed everything else in the hands and timing of God. The mature spiritual guide can do no more or no less.

Selecting Those to Help

It is important to begin this discussion by recognizing the difference between pointing the way and walking alongside a person as a spiritual guide. There are countless times each week when I come across a person who asks me to simply stop for a moment and point the way to Christ for them. They have a question about faith or a challenge in life that motivates them to ask for a bit of help. Whenever I can be helpful, I do stop and point the way. Such moments do not as a rule take a great deal of time, but serve people in important ways. Doing this is part of being a brother in Christ and I am happy to serve.

But walking alongside a person for an extended time as a spiritual guide is another matter. That demands a deeper level of commitment from me, which involves concerted prayer before saying "yes." That level of investment in a person's life will require resources of my time, energy, and spiritual reserves. I must take inventory as to my willingness, availability and ability to serve effectively in this role. One essential part of making that decision is related to assessing the person who is seeking help. Do I believe that he or she is ready to make the necessary commitments to the journey?

Determining a person's readiness to receive spiritual guidance is of utmost importance to me. Over time I have found that there are several things that must be true of the persons I will best be able to serve, including:

- *a hunger to know Christ*
- *a willing and surrendered heart*
- *a teachable spirit*
- *a willingness to be held accountable*
- *personal responsibility*
- *the absence of serious pathology.*

How do I know these qualities are present in those seeking spiritual guidance? I ask questions of them and of the people they know. Before long I am able to have a clear sense of where a person stands relative to each matter, which helps me make a decision about being a spiritual guide for him.

A hunger to know Christ
The spiritual guide must be clear about the help they are to provide to individuals. It is very easy to get sidetracked. People who generally turn to a spiritual guide for help enter that relationship with a wide variety of needs and problems. Often life itself seems to be closing in around them and they are desperate for relief. If the spiritual guide is not careful, sessions can easily shift from spiritual guidance to counseling. Granted, each need is valid, but only one is the central work of the spiritual guide.

Spiritual guidance differs significantly from counseling. Where counseling is problem centered, spiritual guidance is focused on movement toward Christ-likeness. While counseling often looks for root causes and solutions, spiritual guidance is about pursuing Christ and being shaped into His likeness. The counselor often serves from a distance, maintaining professional objectivity. The spiritual guide engages. The spiritual guide must keep faith with this purpose.

The spiritual guide must communicate this to the person he or she serves, evaluating the degree to which the individual is ready and willing to submit to that process. The spiritual guide knows that there is something far more important than solving problems. The key to life is knowing God. When approached properly, problems can become doorways to experiencing the Lord in deeply personal and transforming ways. I am not suggesting that people do not need to deal with their personal problems. I am, however, stating that the person coming for spiritual guidance must know that the pursuit of Christ is the first priority.

Ministry affords many different ways to serve people. Spiritual guidance is focused on what I believe to be the most important of all tasks, helping people move toward Christ. In his book, *Renovation of the Heart: Putting on the Character of Christ*, Dallas Willard states that, "spiritual formation in Christ is the process by which one moves and is moved from self-worship to Christ-centered self-denial as a general condition of life in God's present and eternal kingdom."[4] Spiritual guidance must always serve the movement from self-life to the Christ-centered life.

The spiritual guide must be sure the person seeking help is hungry to move toward Christ and His transforming power. It does not really matter if the person is an honest seeker just beginning the journey toward Jesus or a seasoned follower of the way. The important qualification is that the individual

---

[4] Willard, Dallas, *Renovation of the Heart: Putting on the Character of Christ* (Colorado Springs, Colorado: NavPress, 2002), p. 77.

desires to move forward toward Christ. If so, he is a good candidate for spiritual guidance.

A willing and surrendered heart

Gerald May spent many years serving broken people as a psychiatrist. But his hunger to connect people with God eventually moved him away from medicine to the ministry of spiritual guidance. He came to the conclusion that helping people encounter the wonder and transforming power of God was a higher calling. His many books on spirituality have profoundly affected countless people on the journey toward the Father of love. In *Will and Spirit: A Contemplative Psychology*, May writes about the critical difference between engaging life willingly as opposed to willfully.[5]

Gerald May suggests that willingness is a response that enables a person to surrender to the process of life, allowing it to accomplish the purpose God intended. It is a response based upon the conviction that the "all things" plan of God is real and active in life. God can use the challenges and trials of day-to-day living to transform people into the image of Christ, if people allow that work to take place. Willingness is not easy and in a fallen world far from a natural response to challenges along the way. It is far more likely that a person moves through life willfully, which presents tremendous obstacles to personal change.

Willfulness, according to May, is an attempt to master life for one's own purposes. The willful seek to control, direct and manipulate, not respond with openness and relinquishment. It is easy for me to illustrate this from my own life. As my own dark night began to descend I frantically tried to gain control, desperate to hold on to everything I believed was threatened by the impending storm. I attempted to secure my reputation, ministry, security and sense of self-identity. I was also manic about finding out how long this trial would last and how bad

---

[5]   May, Gerald, *Will and Spirit: A Contemplative Psychology* (New York, New York: HarperCollins, 1982), pp. 5–7.

it might get. This made things worse, feeding and strengthening the very dysfunctions that brought me there in the first place.

Change only began to occur as the Spirit helped me move from willfulness to willingness. Surrender became the path to victory, letting go the step toward freedom. Admittedly I needed help moving from willfulness to willingness, which came in part from my own spiritual guide. But ultimately the shift in attitude was my responsibility. So it is with all who seek spiritual guidance. Individuals must sooner or later be willing to surrender control to the Lord and allow the Spirit to do the work of transformation. It will not happen easily, and in most cases those who say "yes" will not realize what surrender to the "all things" plan of God really means. But the spiritual guide must gain a sense of whether the person seeking help is at least "willing to move toward willingness." Without that shift, as difficult as it may be to make, spiritual guidance is far more likely to lead to increased anger and frustration in an individual's life than it is deep change. And so, sooner better than later, the spiritual guide must hear these words, "with His help, I am willing."

A teachable spirit

I spend a great deal of time in the classroom instructing students about various aspects of Christian ministry. I approach this calling with deep respect, knowing that I have the opportunity to be used of God in shaping precious lives. I desire that every student experience time with me in the classroom as a transformational encounter with God. That means that I must enter the moment fully prepared in the subject matter and open to both the needs of the students and the leading of the Lord. But one other ingredient is necessary if change and growth is to happen. The student must have a teachable spirit. Without that, little movement will take place.

So it is in the ministry of spiritual guidance. It is simply not enough that the spiritual guide enters the moment prepared and attentive. The person seeking guidance must be teachable. I would suggest that four words best define a teachable spirit: *open, attentive, engaged,* and *responsive.* A person who is teachable is open to life as an opportunity to grow, learn new things and experience old things in new ways. People who are open are seldom bored, nor do they "check out" because they have already "heard that before." The teachable person moves into life fully open to the moment, believing that every new day holds rich potential for transforming encounters with God.

A person who is teachable seeks to be attentive in life, with senses alive to their world, their God, and in this case to the spiritual director. They tune in rather than tune out, not wanting to miss what is present in each moment. They watch and they listen. This then demands that a person be fully engaged. A teachable person seeks to move through life attentive to the necessary harmony between body, soul, mind and spirit. He appreciates that being human involves far more than the brain, and commits to feeding and nurturing every aspect of personhood.

Finally, and in some ways most importantly, the teachable person is responsive ... to the journey, to God, and in this case to the spiritual guide. Responsiveness means that a person is willing to submit to the process of growth. The individual who is responsive seeks to embrace events as an opportunity for change. He or she is also aware that to be positioned for transformation, they must be willing to say "yes" to God. Finally, the person seeking spiritual guidance must be responsive to the spiritual guide. Practically, this means seriously considering the advice and direction being offered, as well as accepting and fulfilling the assignments laid out for their personal growth. A teachable spirit is unquestionably a significant qualification to be considered when selecting an individual for spiritual guidance.

A willingness to be held accountable
A person seeking help from a spiritual guide should be willing to be held accountable. It is a necessary and essential part of

spiritual development. Accountability between spiritual guide and follower brings strength to the relationship, enabling a critical integration of guidance, action and growth. With accountability in place, expectations can be clearly articulated and actions evaluated by measures that enhance significant change. The person seeking spiritual guidance needs to willingly accept accountability as part of the work of spiritual guidance.

Accountability that makes a difference happens at two levels. First, the spiritual guide should articulate expectations regarding very basic issues related to spiritual growth. The person seeking help should be expected to come to the scheduled sessions on time, fulfill the assignments set forth by the director and demonstrate serious commitment to the process. The person being helped must be willing to give an account related to such matters when asked, and do so with an attitude that shows that she sees the value of such measures.

There is a second level of accountability that goes much deeper, bringing meaning to spiritual exercises. It is not enough to ask an individual to answer basic questions regarding whether or not he read the Bible, prayed or spent the assigned time journaling that week. The deeper questions are necessary that show the integration of activity with actual spiritual development. The person seeking help must welcome questions such as,

- *Where did you encounter God in Scripture this week?*
- *What do you sense God was seeking to do in your life in the days since we met last?*
- *What feelings did you have when approaching the assigned spiritual disciplines?*
- *What does that tell you about your level of openness, willingness, expectation?*

The spiritual guide should sense an invitation from the follower to press such questions as part of spiritual guidance.

The person seeking help should be willing to answer inquiries that touch areas of struggle and weakness, knowing that attention there is necessary for movement toward Christ and Christ-likeness. Accountability at these levels is part of what it means to be submitted to one another in Christ. Obviously, the spiritual guide needs to exercise accountability in love, respect and sensitivity. He is trying to position an individual for transformation and approaches accountability with that goal clearly in view. The person seeking help must be willing to enter a relationship of accountability if he has any hope that the process of spiritual guidance will truly position him for lasting change. To the spiritual guide, this qualification must be a non-negotiable.

Personal responsibility
Accountability and responsibility are really two sides of the same coin. Where accountability invites measurement, personal responsibility places the obligation to properly respond to life where it truly belongs: squarely upon the individual seeking help. Spiritual guidance does not in any way mean that the actions of the spiritual guide singularly determine the amount of growth that occurs in the person who is seeking guidance. The role of the spiritual guide is to help another person assume that responsibility for himself, helping the individual exercise personal initiative that positions him for the transforming work of the Lord. The spiritual guide is certainly responsible to provide sound guidance, but the responses that truly translate into growth rest with the individual. That includes responsibility for his actions, attitudes, feelings, weaknesses, strengths, expectations and commitments in life.

There have been times when I have had individuals grow frustrated with my spiritual guidance, stating that they were not satisfied with the movement they were experiencing in their relationship with the Lord. I am well aware that any such critique warrants serious examination on my part, to see if I am guiding people in ways that best serve the process. But there are also occasions when the problem lies with the person seeking help. What some people really want is for me to accept responsibility for their growth, making it my fault if change does not occur, all the while refusing to personally engage in the journey.

I once had a person tell me that he was not sensing the Lord's presence in his life, blaming me for not being helpful, even though he resisted positioning himself before the Lord in prayer. I am fully committed to reasonably doing what I can to support a person on the journey to Christ, providing instruction, help and assignments designed to initiate change. But that individual is alone responsible for the amount and degree of change that is ultimately possible in his life. When I stand before the Lord in eternity to give an account for my life, no one but I will be held responsible for my actions or my growth while on earth. While I must be accountable to others, I am the sole person responsible for me. Accepting personal responsibility is part of adulthood and the person seeking help from a spiritual guide needs to understand that.

The absence of serious pathology

The effective spiritual guide must know the limits of her expertise and gifting. Nowhere is that more important than when it involves people who suffer from significant emotional and mental disorders. There are individuals, good Christian people, who have levels of personal dysfunction that truly make it difficult for them to function normally in life. Granted, we all have some degree of emotional turmoil and our own annoying imbalances. But for some dear people, the tendency to act out and respond to life in dysfunctional ways actually disorders their world. They can have trouble maintaining relationships, reacting to people in inappropriate and destructive ways and totally misread what is happening around them. These broken people are part of every congregation and often demand a great deal of attention from those in leadership.

There are a wide variety of causes for emotional and mental disorders, ranging from biochemical imbalances, to childhood wounding, to adult trauma, to sustained duress in an individual's life situation, to significant spiritual bondage. Regardless of the cause, the issues are often complex and the behaviors that accompany them difficult to handle. Working with such individuals demands a level of understanding and skill that is beyond what most people have who choose to serve as spiritual guides. Education and experience in the behavioral sciences at some meaningful level is needed.

A person who struggles with significant pathology is certainly dearly loved of the Lord and needs the acceptance, understanding and support of the community of faith. The embrace of other believers is vitally important to the healing journey. But such an individual also needs the help of a person who understands the complexities of mental and emotional upheaval, which ultimately means this: the spiritual guide must accept the limits of his expertise and refer those who need greater help to someone who is able to walk them toward freedom. Such an attitude should never be interpreted as somehow limiting God's ability to work through someone as they reach out to help another person. This discussion is about being a responsible steward of gifts and limitations, so that people in need are well served by the body of Christ.[6]

I end this discussion where it began. Serving as a spiritual guide is serious business with the potential to profoundly help another person move forward on the journey to Christlikeness. The mature spiritual guide should understand that

---

[6] I am careful to identify behaviors that suggest more serious dysfunction in an individual's life. I always encourage people to be aware of significant mood swings, the inability to maintain relationships, inordinate seasons of fear and anxiety, unusual avoidance behaviors, the inability to maintain proper boundaries, extreme emotional reactions to loss or trial, self-mutilating and radical shifts in personality. These could be indications of serious pathology and should be watched. Laypersons would find the book *Behind the Masks*, written by Wayne E. Oates and published by Westminster John Knox press quite helpful to this discussion.

the relationship she has with a person seeking help demands a high level of commitment and responsibility from both parties. As such, the spiritual guide should prayerfully consider who they are willing to yoke with for the journey. Selecting the right person at the right time is very important to the process. The discussion here was intended to help that process, knowing all the while that in the end, it is the Spirit of Christ who leads the way. In the next chapter attention will be given to several essential resources that the spiritual guide must have to effectively serve people on the journey of life.

Chapter 4

Essential Resources for the Spiritual Guide

David Hall is one of my dearest friends. He grew up in the mountains of Idaho and is as rugged as they come. He loves to hunt, fish, mountain climb, do construction, horseback ride and play sports, wholeheartedly. Life around him is seldom safe, but it sure is fun. There is a wildness to David that makes being with him a constant challenge and adventure. But David is also one of the most caring, gentle, attentive pastors I have ever been around. He is able to anticipate need like no one else I know. Somehow he can walk into a room and hurting people immediately know he cares. The lonely find a friend, the distraught a listening ear and the confused a gentle guide. David's combination of strength and sensitivity is amazing to experience. It has healing power.

On many occasions David and I, along with several other friends, have ventured into the high mountains for days at a time. While there are many wonderful stories to be shared, one important point stands out related to the discussion of spiritual guidance. David and I enter the moment of adventure from completely opposite directions. David Hall spends weeks preparing for every trip. To him, the process of preparation is as important and fun as the journey itself. He gathers every possible piece of equipment, plans the journey down to the finest detail, anticipates the unexpected, and arrives centered and ready to go.

I on the other hand consistently wait to the very last minute, throw what I think I might need into a cardboard box and set off for the rendezvous site. Invariably I forget more than one important item, like a fishing pole on an angling adventure, or hiking boots for climbing, or my sleeping bag. I tend to arrive in a whirl and can be more than a bit irritating to David. Sooner or later I end up needing something I have forgotten to bring and thank God my friend pulls through. In fact, over the years he has come to anticipate my inattention to such detail and brings along what he is sure I will forget. His faithfulness to my weakness makes a great difference.

There is an important lesson to be learned here for the spiritual guide. Never start out on the adventure without adequate preparation and the necessary resources. Jesus once told two parables that every spiritual guide should take seriously (Luke 14:28–33). Christ was teaching His followers about the cost of following Him in life and wanted each disciple to be prepared for what they would eventually face in ministry. Jesus illustrated His point by reflecting upon a builder and a king. He emphasized in each parable the importance of adequate preparation and resourcing before setting out on an important task.

Jesus told the disciples that a wise builder considers the full cost of construction before building so that he is sure to complete what he started. The builder would not want to lay a foundation and then lack the resources to finish the job. He would look foolish. Likewise, a king considering war must accurately assess the power of the enemy before entering a battle. Otherwise, the king might send armies out against a much greater enemy and once engaged, lose all power to negotiate. Jesus had long before anticipated the Boy Scout motto, "Be Prepared."

Like any adventure, serving as a spiritual guide for someone on the journey toward Christ requires preparation and resources. The terrain will be difficult, the obstacles formidable, and the changing seasons of life threatening. Adequate nourishment is essential, as is the necessary first-aid kit for the inevitable injury along the way. And unquestionably the spiritual guide must know how to set a true course toward the final destination, remembering that Christ is, for all journeys, the believer's "true north".

It is not the intention of this discussion to list every resource available to the effective spiritual guide. This chapter focuses upon four foundational resources that are invaluable to the ministry of spiritual guidance:

- *the presence of the Holy Spirit*
- *the authority of the spiritual guide*
- *the support of Christ's community*
- *the living Word of God.*

The spiritual guide should never attempt to lead a person a single step forward without knowing these resources are immediately at his or her disposal. They are each that vital to the journey.

The Presence of the Holy Spirit

Jesus made one point crystal clear to the disciples. They were not to attempt ministry in their own strength! Throughout His life on earth Jesus moved in the power of the Holy Spirit and taught the same principle to His disciples. Christ was born of the Spirit, consecrated by the Spirit and empowered by the Holy Spirit to bring healing and redemption to the world. He told His followers that the Spirit was key to life (John 6:63), and said that the Holy Spirit would flow forth from believers like a stream of living water (John 7:38). As Jesus prepared to return to glory He promised the Holy Spirit's coming to help the disciples fulfill the mission of the Kingdom (John 14:16). Jesus called the Holy Spirit the Comforter, Counselor and Spirit of Truth. He said that the Spirit would guide the disciples (John 16:13), remind them of everything Jesus said (John 14:26), and bear witness to Jesus Christ in every way (John 15:26).

When Jesus met with the disciples following the resurrection He breathed upon them, saying, *"Receive the Holy
Spirit"* (John 20:22). And on the day of His resurrection Jesus
commanded His followers to wait for the baptism of the Holy
Spirit before they took one step forward in ministry. He
promised them that the Spirit's coming would bring Kingdom
power to their lives (Acts 1:4–8). And wait the disciples did.
For weeks they gathered together behind locked doors and
prayed. Then suddenly, with gale force the Holy Spirit out-
rageously blew into their lives and set them aflame with the
presence of God. They spilled into the streets, sharing the
message of Christ with boldness and the church was born
with power (Acts 2:1–47).

What follows in the record of the church in Acts is
absolutely awe-inspiring. The disciples were used of the
Holy Spirit to work signs and wonders throughout the then
civilized world. The sick were healed, the lame walked, those
in demonic bondage were set free and the dead were raised to
new life. When the lost encountered the Spirit's power they
transferred loyalty from the kingdom of darkness to the
Kingdom of light and life. Paul identified demonstrations of
the Holy Spirit's power as foundational to the Christian life
(1 Corinthians 2:1–4). He also admonished followers of all
time to be repeatedly filled with the Holy Spirit in order to
move through life as Christ intended (Ephesians 5:18).

The Holy Spirit is far more than a theological category to be
discussed like a topic of some time long ago. He is, as Saint
John of the Cross said, the Flame of Love, seeking to ignite
all who desire with the fire of God's presence. He is God at
work in the lives of believers, indwelling, nurturing, gifting
and empowering those who are open for Kingdom life and
ministry. Far too many Christians and countless local
churches have marginalized the ministry of the Holy Spirit.
They do this either out of ignorance or an unbiblical desire to
limit how He would manifest His presence in their lives or
ministries. What results is a powerless Christianity that
attracts few and changes even fewer.

The spiritual guide can not afford to minimize the Holy Spirit in his life, instead welcoming Him to move in and through him to the glory of Christ. The power that the Holy Spirit brings into that relationship, and the gifts that He gives for service, are absolutely essential to helping another person move toward Christ. There will be difficult times and challenges along the way that will demand far more than mere human effort can provide. The journey will involve times of oppression and opposition from spiritual forces bent on destruction. The spiritual guide will unquestionably need help. When welcomed, the Holy Spirit becomes Counselor, Comforter, Guide and Teacher to both the spiritual guide and the person seeking guidance. His presence along the journey can be experienced personally, dynamically, and in ways that lead to deep change and transformation.

There is a radical difference between living the Christian life in the power of the flesh and experiencing it in the power of the Holy Spirit. While the challenges and trials of the journey do not change, life along the way certainly does. There comes a vitality and intimacy to faith that flows straight from the Kingdom of God. At times the Spirit is experienced as a gentle breeze, and yet there are other moments when the Holy Spirit moves through with hurricane force. Like wind itself, the Holy Spirit can not be controlled or captured within a box for examination. He is alive, powerful and willing to move in and through all who extend an honest welcome to His presence.

The Lord assured His followers that the Father desired to give the Holy Spirit to all who ask (Luke 11:13). Those who do, soon find that the Father is most generous, giving far beyond what one could ask or think. Once touched by the presence of the Holy Spirit there will be no turning back for the spiritual guide or the person seeking help. Each will be hooked for life. Calvin Miller discussed the Holy Spirit's ministry in his book, *Into the Depths with God*. Commenting upon the outpouring of the Holy Spirit upon people, Miller wrote,

"Heady inebriation this: Spirit intoxication. It is a glorious addiction. If we but take one sip, we Pneumaholics must have more of the Pneuma ... we are alive and the life is in the wind and the fire."[7]

It is my prayer that the spiritual guide acquires a lifetime thirst for the New Wine of the Precious Spirit of Christ.

The Authority of the Spiritual Guide

The religious leaders of Christ's day were constantly challenging the Lord's authority to say and do what He did. They did not question that He ministered with power. The scribes, Pharisees and priests saw the results of His healing touch right before their eyes. Sick people were being healed, the blind and handicapped restored, the demonized delivered and the leprous made clean. But none of this turned the religious leaders into followers of Jesus. The content of the Lord's message and His refusal to submit to the religious biases of that time, infuriated the religious community. They saw that Jesus neither recognized nor bowed to their authority, which was a great affront to them.

Regardless of the miracles that Christ was performing, the scribes, Pharisees and priests rejected Christ and His ministry. They only recognized those leaders who held authority based in the religious institution of their day. Someone needed to have the proper title, office, robe and responsibility in order to exercise religious power. No one held power unless they dispensed it to them. And the power being exercised was political and religious, requiring a strictly enforced law in order to be maintained. This type of religious authority may have looked impressive, but it did very little to bring transformation to people's lives.

The common people of Christ's day did not question the authority of Jesus. They were amazed by it and they flocked to

---

[7] Miller, Calvin, *Into the Depths with God*, p. 127.

hear Him teach and watch Him minister as no one had before in their midst. His words held power that changed lives, which they desperately longed to experience. The people of Christ's day felt the full weight of dark oppression and were beaten down by it. They found in Christ a man who could actually do something about it. The people were positively stunned when diseases and demons submitted to His words. Jesus held no title or office, yet when He spoke amazing things happened. Even unseen forces submitted to Jesus, fully aware that He was acting under the authority of God Himself.

The spiritual guide must address the question of authority in relationship to his ministry. What right does the spiritual guide have to help others along the path? Who recognizes the call and gifting of the spiritual guide to set them apart for this type of service to other Christians? It is easy for someone to set himself apart as a spiritual guide, but by what authority do they do this? The answers to these questions are very important, not only for the person seeking help, but for the spiritual guide as well.

I am concerned about the question of authority as it relates to all ministry, not just spiritual guidance. Every day I spend time with men and women who are preparing for vocational Christian ministry. Some will be going into pastoral ministries, others counseling, and a few each year move on to teaching posts. They spend years in training, experience internships, often connect themselves to denominational leaders, and eventually move out in ministry. A great deal of time and hard work has gone into their preparation to serve the Lord. And usually they graduate with skills and competencies well developed for the tasks that lie ahead.

With graduation comes a degree, which is usually followed by an appointment to some official position, title, and clearly defined role. And while each of these may have some level of importance, it is critical that a person never sees them as the locus of authority in his life. Granted, there may come with these things a certain degree of bureaucratic authority, but alone that does not give a person authority in Kingdom matters. That true locus of authority rests with Christ and Him alone. Degrees do not carry great weight in spiritual matters. Preparation for ministry does matter and as such I am fully committed to and supportive of education. But in the heavenly realms, what counts is a person's relationship with Jesus Christ.

Authority in the Kingdom of God is based upon five key realities that must be true of a person seeking to serve the Lord. An individual must be in an intimate relationship with Christ, maturing toward Christ-likeness, called and gifted for specific ministry, empowered by the Holy Spirit, and moving forward under the authority of His reign. These characteristics are recognized in heaven and carry great weight when exercised in the work of ministry on earth. Scripture says that believers sit with Christ in heavenly realms, which is clear evidence that the authority that truly matters flows from the throne of God (Ephesians 2:6).

Luke recorded a very important story about authority involving Jesus and His disciples (Luke 10:1–24). The Lord sent seventy-two followers out into surrounding areas to preach the gospel and heal the sick. When they returned to Christ they were overcome with joy and excitement. They saw demons and diseases respond to their command. Jesus rejoiced with them, assuring each that He had given them that authority, which was directly linked to their relationship with Him. Christians today can and must still minister in the authority of Jesus Christ. Believers are positioned with Him in heaven and as such have the right to teach, preach, serve and guide as His workers, duly appointed and powerfully supported from on high.

It is critical that the spiritual guide does not become enamored with degrees, titles and official positions as the bases of authority. It is a subtle shift in priority that can lead to the same dead religiosity that it did in Christ's day. Confidence in Christ and submission to the power of the Kingdom is the key to helping people move toward Christ. The spiritual guide, while gentle and loving toward those seeking help, must move ahead with boldness in the calling Christ has extended and in the gifts He has given through the Holy Spirit.

Those who move under Christ's authority soon see that there is little need for public recognition. Having or not having a title means little to the process. People will seek such a spiritual guide out for help because they sense the movement of God in the person's life. They will see that people under the spiritual guide's care move forward and are transformed by the power of Christ. They will recognize that there is spiritual power present in the spiritual guide's ministry. That is the authority that should matter most to any responsible spiritual guide. Having said all this, the spiritual guide cannot assume that he has the right to serve simply because he believes he is moving under the authority of Christ. The Lord's body, the community of believers, must see that relationship and calling in a person's life, and agree.

The Support of Christ's Community

The woman who approached me after the first day of my class on spiritual formation appeared to be in her mid-thirties. She patiently waited as other students requested information about aspects of the course, then asked to speak to me privately. I agreed and the two of us stepped to the side of the classroom where no one could hear. She introduced herself and then said, "I am the most important person you will ever meet in your life. I am a prophetess of the Lord and I have been sent here by angels to tell you something. You can learn a lot from me." I am sure that the look on my face gave away how taken aback I was by her words. I had many thoughts rushing through my mind, yet I thanked her for telling me that.

I then asked her a question. "Who vouches for you and your ministry?" The young lady did not seem to understand what I was asking, so I approached the question another way. "Where do you go to church and what pastor can I contact about your claims to walk in prophetic gifting?" I did not suggest that I discounted her claims, though that thought was taking shape in my mind, but I did want her to know that I was under no obligation to accept what she said at face value. The student did not like what I was suggesting and started to explain that I was resisting the Holy Spirit. But I pressed the point with her kindly and asked again about her connection to the body of Christ. She eventually told me where she attended church and gave me the name of a pastor who would vouch for her. And with that she left.

During that week I called and talked to her pastor. I shared that I was not closed to the Lord working in this way, but had my doubts about this person's maturity. The pastor told me that not only did he share that concern, the church had asked her to please stop giving prophecies to people, because she was not under anyone's authority, nor were her words reaping fruit for the Kingdom. Thanking the pastor, I ended the conversation knowing I was about to face a great challenge. Somehow, I needed to lovingly influence this person to connect to the body of Christ, so that others could nurture, nourish and guide her life properly.

Ministering in the power and authority of Christ must never be done in isolation from the community of Jesus Christ. Regardless of how skilled, experienced and mature a spiritual guide might be, they are called of Christ to stay attached to others who are moving toward Christ. Jesus lived and ministered in the context of community and so must every one of His followers. The spiritual guide who ministers in isolation from other believers risks imbalance, spiritual deception and potential destruction at the hands of the evil one.

If the destination of life is Christ-likeness, then commitment to community is one of its central characteristics. A person cannot be like Jesus without committing to journey with others through life. From eternity past Christ has taken part in the beautiful, social co-existence of the Godhead. Love, celebration, joy, wonder and eternal creativity are expressed within the communal life of the Trinity. When

Jesus came to earth He invited His followers to join in that corporate dance. He not only called the disciples to Himself, but He called them to one another, repeatedly affirming the connection that characterizes Christian brothers and sisters.

The spiritual guide must have this kind of connection in the community of Christ. The level of relationship the spiritual guide has with other mature believers must go far beyond formality, pressing the depths of intimacy where the true self is free to develop and grow. A caring Christ-centered community should provide the context where the spiritual guide first discovers and develops his calling to lead others on the journey of life. The community of Christ should affirm that call and provide the support and environment necessary to spiritual growth and maturity. The spiritual guide should experience a sense of being sent forth from the community to serve Christ, and then received back again for refreshment and refocusing.

The spiritual guide needs the resource of community to help others journey to Christ. The ongoing encouragement and prayer support is invaluable to responsible spiritual guidance. The community of the spiritual guide must also exercise a healthy sense of oversight and accountability, lovingly making sure than the spiritual guide is taking care of themselves as they help others toward Christ. And when tired or hurt along the way, it should be the community of Christ that nurtures renewal and healing to the servant of the Lord.

The spiritual guide also must help the person they guide to embrace community with the same deep resolve. By modeling and guiding, the Christian follower should be encouraged to engage with other believers for learning, growth, worship, celebration and service. There is strength and healing available to believers when the community of Christ meets together. People who are desperate for Christ need to discover that He is often found where the two and three gather in His name (Matthew 18:20). The spiritual guide must make community a non-negotiable part of the Christian life and do all that is necessary to help others do the same.

The Living Word of God

The Pursuit of God, by A.W. Tozer, is a classic of Christian literature. It has been read by millions of people world wide and is known for its deep, biblical spirituality. Reading it is a transformational encounter in itself, drawing people into a rich experience of the living God. What few know is that Tozer was motivated to write this volume, at least in part, because of his concern with what he called biblical preachers. A.W. Tozer felt that many men were claiming to be faithful to Scripture, yet preached the Bible in ways that did not bring the listener into contact with the presence of God. He insisted that preaching which was fully faithful to Scripture brought with it an encounter with Christ Himself, not just information about Him. Tozer believed that such an experience of God was foundational to being a Christian. He insisted that rightly declaring the Word of God would draw others into a deep, intimate relationship with the Father.

Many people today have been taught to go to Scripture for the discovery of propositional truth. They attempt to use all the skills and tools available to, as many say, "rightly divide the Word." Unfortunately, their approach seems more like dissecting than dividing, pulling and picking away at a text in an effort to discover the meaning of each part. They treat the Word of God as something to be handled by the reader, pawed at until the Scripture reluctantly surrenders its meaning. A fundamental principle of this method is that only the skilled student of the Bible is capable of comprehending its meaning. Somehow, in the end the text has lost its life-giving power.

I understand the importance of biblical scholarship. But I am convinced that the Bible is the Living Word of God with a purpose far greater than dispensing information and standards of Christian living. Scripture is inspired with the presence of the Holy Spirit and the deepest truth of any text is only revealed when the Holy Spirit reveals it. The Word of God is empowered to handle the reader far more than be handled by one. The person who submits to the presence of God in His Word is forever changed by the encounter. They find that they are in fact the object of the moment, not the Bible. And God's Word has the power to cut straight to the center of the human heart, just like a two-edged sword (Hebrews 4:12). Read the Scripture from that perspective and it is far from a boring exercise. It becomes a transforming moment in the presence of the Living Christ. As for me, I need far more transformation than information anyway!

The spiritual guide must invest significant amounts of time encountering the Lord in Scripture. It should be the first place he goes and the place he stays the longest. He should approach the Bible surrendered to the Holy Spirit's presence, seeking to not only know what the text says, but to experience the power of God present within those sacred words. Bible reading is not first and foremost about acquiring information. It is a discipline of personal transformation whenever the reader allows all her natural and spiritual senses to be surrendered to the Spirit in the moment. The spiritual guide who engages the Scriptures like this will find reserves of spiritual capital un-mined by most readers.

The effective spiritual guide must introduce those he helps to the transformational reading of God's Word. Seekers should be taught to approach God's Word surrendered to the revealing presence of the Holy Spirit. They should be instructed to move slowly through the Word, attentive to every spiritual movement that is attached to it. The spiritual guide should teach those being helped that how much a text covers them is far more important than how many texts they cover while reading. It is not speed that is essential, but anticipation, silence, listening, waiting and receiving the message that God has in the moment. The spiritual guide should bring this way of embracing Scripture into the sessions of spiritual guidance, modeling what it means to be open to the presence of the Living Christ found in the Word of the Almighty God.

The day of journey comes quickly for the spiritual guide and often with unanticipated challenge. He will always do well to stay richly supplied with the resources so essential to the task. The effective spiritual guide must prioritize personal growth and maturity in each of the matters discussed in this chapter. He should stay constant in prayer for more of the Holy Spirit's presence, persevering like the friend at midnight until the Father arises to meet that cry (Luke 11:5–8). From there, the spiritual guide must grow in authority, all the while connected to the community of believers who nurture and support his ministry to the Kingdom. And unquestionably, the spiritual guide must establish a rhythm to life that includes daily seasons in the Word of God. Practical steps to developing resources like these are steps well taken.

Chapter 5

Where and When Does Spiritual Guidance Take Place?

I have often wondered what it would be like to receive spiritual direction from one of the giants of the faith. Imagine spending an entire day asking questions about deep spiritual matters to Paul, or Peter, or John the Beloved. Or listening to Augustine or Athanasius speak about the realities of the Kingdom of God. I cannot even fathom what it would be like to sit with Madam Guyon, Francois Fenelon, John Wesley, or Jonathan Edwards, and listen to them speak of Jesus. Contemporaries like Howard Thurman, Henri Nouwen, A.W. Tozer, and David Watson are but a few of many names that come to mind when I daydream about learning from those who have walked the journey with Jesus. I know that such opportunities will not happen for me. What makes me all the more thankful is that they each took the time to write down their thoughts for those who would follow.

What must it have been like for the disciples to actually follow Jesus? Their experience of spiritual guidance was as intense as it gets. For three years they spent virtually every moment with the Lord. Every day held the potential for direction, teaching, observing and experiencing Kingdom principles. The disciples traveled with Christ, listened as He preached, watched Him work signs and wonders and saw how He responded to those who were opposing Him. They then were able to sit alone with Jesus as He debriefed the events of the day, receiving insights and instructions that others did not get.

If Jesus told a crowd of people a parable, like the story of the sower and the seed (Matthew 13:1–23), He later helped the disciples understand it. When He taught Kingdom truths, like He did about the rich having a difficult time entering heaven (Luke 18:18–30), they were able to ask questions for further clarification. If the disciples reacted to rejection improperly, as when James and John wanted to call fire down upon the Samaritans (Luke 9:51–56), they had Jesus there to teach them the way of love. As they began to position themselves for places of power (Mark 10:35–45), the disciples received immediate direction and guidance from the Lord about the nature of servanthood. All of life became the context for intense spiritual direction for the disciples and they were forever changed by the three years they walked with Jesus.

On one level none of us will receive spiritual guidance from Jesus, nor will many of us have opportunity to sit at the feet of the Christian leaders of history. It may seem like a nice dream, but it is really more of an unrealizable fantasy. But that does not mean that the insights of the saints of the past and the principles of Christ's direction cannot become part of the spiritual guidance people receive today. The effective spiritual guide can set a format for helping others that, while certainly having limits, can position people for great change and personal transformation. There is much that Jesus did that the spiritual director can include in his or her work with people. He or she can also integrate insights from those who have walked before into a format for direction that is effective, practical for most people, and workable for the spiritual guide. The material that follows in this and the next chapter will focus upon the format and content of meaningful spiritual guidance.

Establishing the Best Format for Spiritual Guidance

It would be helpful to briefly highlight once again the nature and purpose of spiritual direction. As discussed in chapter 2, I define the work of a spiritual guide as the process of helping others respond to the journey of life in ways that invite personal transformation into the image of Jesus Christ. As mentioned earlier, spiritual guidance happens over time. It is focused on helping others understand and respond to life events in ways that position them for deep change. The spiritual guide does not make choices for people, but instead helps them make the choices that give room for the Holy Spirit's ministry of personal transformation. The spiritual guide seeks to equip the person being helped with the skills and tools that will best serve movement toward Christ-likeness.

With this focus in mind, the spiritual guide should prayerfully consider the format of spiritual direction that will be most effective. Again, the possibility of establishing the level of intensity in spiritual guidance reflected in the ministry of Christ is unlikely for most people. Granted there are retreat experiences and some events at monasteries that endeavor to replicate such a format. But most people cannot participate in that type of opportunity for spiritual growth. There are, however, practical options for spiritual guidance that are workable for most every follower of Christ and are proven to be effective and efficient ways to help others on the journey.

The spiritual guide should develop a strategy for guidance that best fits the needs of the people he serves. Again, the choices the spiritual guide makes related to such matters must be prayerfully considered, for there are special pluses inherent in each option. The discussion that follows is highly practical, yet points to unique opportunities for the Holy Spirit to touch a person's life.

Official or unofficial

When I became a new pastor thirty years ago, I was assigned a spiritual guide by the denominational leadership. This relationship was a requisite of entering pastoral ministry and an officially designated part of my training as a first-year member of that ecclesiastical group. The spiritual guide was an older man who had been in pastoral ministry many years. He was responsible to help me acclimate to the call of ministry, caring for my soul as I sought to care for the spiritual lives of those in the local church I pastored. My appointed spiritual guide was required to observe how I did the work of ministry and respond to its challenges. He paid attention to not only my strengths and gifts, but also my attitudes and reactions along the way.

Our relationship covered the span of one year, during which we were instructed to meet together and talk regularly. He had been schooled in his responsibilities, so he knew what was expected by denominational leaders. I in turn understood that this relationship was not optional and that my willingness and surrender had significant consequences for my future. Records of our time together were kept and the appropriate reports made to those who were in leadership. I was blessed to be served by a wonderful man who showed deep care for my soul. I eventually asked him to stand for my ordination, which was an honor to us both.

There are definite advantages to an official relationship between spiritual guide and the guided, particularly when serious issues, such as the competency to minister, are at stake. Both parties tend to take the time they spend seriously, recognizing that there are ultimately consequences involved. This can and should lead to a level of faithfulness and diligence that is valuable to the process.

But there are also great advantages to an unofficial relationship that must be considered by the spiritual guide. People who enlist for spiritual direction without official sanction or requirement are being motivated by their own desire for change and personal growth. They tend to come ready to work and willing to follow. They have spent some time considering who to ask for spiritual guidance and are more likely to move toward trust much sooner. There is a spontaneity to the unofficial relationship that lends itself to transforming encounters with life. Official relationships are often agenda driven, and while that is certainly not a bad thing, it can be limiting.

Most importantly, an unofficial relationship tends to provide a context for honesty and vulnerability. Weaknesses are more openly discussed, failures more likely to be revealed, and needs more consistently touched. Official relationships are limited in this respect because other issues are often at stake. People in official relationships tend to be far more selective in what they share, which in the end impedes progress toward the greater goal of Christ-likeness. The spiritual guide must prayerfully weigh the format that best fits each person seeking guidance.

Formal or informal

For most people I serve in spiritual guidance I am simply Terry, a brother in Christ who has agreed to help them on the journey to Christ. I do not display my diplomas, point to the books I have written on the subject, or present myself as any kind of authority on spiritual guidance. I am, while deeply engaged, casual, informal, and as laid back as possible. But to others who come for spiritual guidance, I insist on being Dr Wardle. I select a stance of spiritual guidance that is formal and involves a level of professionalism and authority.

The choice between formal and informal must never be about the personal preference, comfort zone, or ego needs of the spiritual guide. The decision between establishing a formal or informal stance for direction is made in prayer based upon the guidance of the Lord and the needs of the person being served. It is, as always, about enhancing the person's movement to Christ and His likeness.

People who come for spiritual guidance after being greatly wounded by authority figures in the past, and/or enter the relationship with debilitating feelings of insecurity, are often served best by an informal approach. The level of anxiety they feel toward those in authority would make movement very difficult. If the spiritual guide is able to descend from any and all vestiges power, and caringly serve a wounded person in humility, healing and growth will be far more likely. The spiritual guide would become a member of Jesus' order of the towel and basin, washing the feet of the broken in ways that lead to deep transforming encounters with the Holy Spirit.

There will be times though when the spiritual guide must establish a level of formality with those being served. There will be people who seek spiritual direction who will, in their own brokenness, try to build an unhealthy dependency upon the spiritual guide. They will want to have access to the private world of the spiritual guide, subconsciously seeking to establish an unhealthy codependency. For the welfare of both the spiritual guide and those being helped, this must never happen. Boundaries must be maintained at all times. Also, the spiritual guide will encounter those who are rebellious of authority, showing deep disrespect and contempt for leadership. Once again, the spiritual guide should choose a stance of formality, demanding respect for themselves and the process of spiritual guidance itself.

Directive or non-directive
The adage that no one likes to be told what to do is simply not true. I have met many people who come for spiritual direction who want me to give step-by-step instructions on how to respond to life, even down to the simplest of choices. It is as if they want me to serve as a spiritual palm reader. They expect that I will lay out life for them so that they have to take no personal responsibility for their choices. Whether based in insecurity or irresponsibility, the goal is the same for such persons. They do not want to take the risk and choose for themselves. And in cases like that, I regularly choose a non-directive stance of spiritual direction, to the general displeasure of such people.

The spiritual guide must be compassionate toward those

who are either afraid or unwilling to choose. This type of dysfunction is painful and runs very deep into a person's soul, caused by deep wounds that need the healing touch of Christ. The spiritual guide should care deeply and stay in the pain with the person as they learn to take responsibility. That is not easy for a spiritual guide, especially when the proper choice seems so obvious. But in such cases, helping people grow confident and choose responses to life for themselves is even more important than the choices they initially make.

But once again, what works best for one person may not be the most helpful format for another. There is something to be said for the spiritual discipline of submitting to another person. Directive spiritual guidance should never be a lifelong stance that a spiritual guide takes with a person, but it does have its place. Submission in the body of Christ is an important part of growth. It is an aspect of willingness and surrender. The spiritual guide should expect the person seeking help to do the activities, spiritual exercises, and disciplines assigned. If they do not, the spiritual guide has a right to know why. And in some cases, when it best serves the process, there will need to be consequences. Saint Francis would at times require that a novice and seasoned friar reverse roles as they went on a journey. The young man was in authority and the older required to submit to his leadership. Saint Francis believed this taught each a great deal about the importance of authority and submission.

Scheduled or unscheduled
Spiritual guidance happens best, especially initially, when there is a scheduled rhythm to the meetings between spiritual guide and those seeking help. This enhances progress significantly, allowing for disciplines and activities to be assigned to individuals, knowing that there will be discussion and accountability following. The spiritual guide should prayerfully determine how often he should meet with a particular person and over what period of time. There is really no rule

about frequency or duration. I prefer in most cases to meet no more than monthly with people, allowing enough of life to occur to provide points for reflection and discussion. Since so much of spiritual guidance is about developing skills and tools for spiritual growth, time in between sessions is critical to engaging what is learned in day-to-day events.

Scheduled sessions serve the process in other ways as well. It gives the spiritual guide an opportunity to lay out a plan, preparing to help the individual over an extended period of time. It not only is practical for both the spiritual guide and guided to work with a predetermined schedule, it also puts discipline into the routine for the person seeking help.

But there are times when I move beyond a predetermined schedule to meet with people as the need arises. As a rule, I only do this with people who have been in direction for some time, and are now moving toward more informal, non-directive spiritual guidance. In most cases, unscheduled spiritual direction occurs in response to certain life events that people need to process. I limit my availability to do this, because I do not want my own schedule to be driven by the unscheduled events in another person's life. But there are times, when such moments are windows of tremendous opportunity and I gladly step into them with others.

Individual or group

In many ways this section should read *Individual and Group*, because both formats offer such wonderful opportunities for transforming encounters with Christ. The advantages of individual spiritual direction seem obvious. Attention can be given exclusively to one person. Every session, conversation, event and assignment can be shaped to directly impact that one person. The lessons and exercises employed can be pinpoint accurate and relevant to the journey he or she is making through life. And if the person generally gets lost in groups, finding it difficult to engage and be heard, individual spiritual direction is an important first format for change.

But in our society "individual" turns into "individualism" far too easily. Even the Christian seems predisposed to move to the beat of his or her own drummer, regardless of what others may be experiencing in life. That is not the way of Christ, who engaged in community as a context for spiritual growth. Group spiritual guidance is an exciting format for encountering the Holy Spirit. While I am not naturally drawn to group experiences, I have seen the power of community at work and I am now a deeply committed believer. Jesus does come where two and three gather and lives are radically changed.

Group spiritual direction provides many participants with their first experience of life in community. Everyone needs to have a place of belonging and acceptance, and the spiritual guide can initiate that through group guidance. The format for group sessions must be balanced between a predetermined agenda for discussion, experience and activity, with opportunities for individuals to process their thoughts and feelings. The spiritual guide must have skills in group dynamics to best accomplish this. The spiritual guide will soon see that when people journey together, support, love, care and encouragement begin to flow. People learn from each other, and help one another stay positioned for the transforming work of the Holy Spirit on the journey to Christ-likeness.

Compensated or uncompensated

The issue of money and the church is always a sensitive one. Abuse and mismanagement have made more than a few people suspicious about how those people in vocational ministry handle finances. There are individuals who reject the idea that a person should be paid for what he does in service to the church. The spiritual guide must come to a place of peace about whether there will be any compensation for services rendered for spiritual guidance. Settling that matter personally should happen long before the spiritual guide begins helping other people.

Individuals who are appointed to a position on a church staff are often able to make spiritual guidance part of what they do for the compensation they receive from a congregation. Others, like me, choose to reserve the right of compensation on a case-by-case basis. Years of training and the qualification that accompanies certain degree programs, make this easier for some than others. But the scriptural admonition that a workman is worthy of his hire relates directly to this issue (1 Timothy 5:18). I believe that qualified Christians are free to make the choice that fits their calling and response to the Lord's leading. I have more than a few friends who have every reason to seek compensation for services, yet choose not to because of personal conviction.

The matter of compensation does have ramifications for spiritual growth and development. People who have never experienced the beauty and generosity of grace often need to receive spiritual guidance as a gift. Being given something so valuable for free can point people to the matchless generosity of Christ. It is also important for those who have trouble receiving grace gifts, who are caught in the destructive cycle of needing to earn and deserve everything that comes their way. The spiritual guide should serve the Lord by doing what is best for a person's spiritual development with reference to this issue.

Conversely, there are people who need to compensate the spiritual guide because it is good for their journey to Christ. Whether through money, or services, they should be encouraged to pay for the care they receive. For many people, doing this motivates them to value what they receive all the more. Many take the sessions and assignments seriously because they are required to compensate the spiritual guide. Money means something to most people and they tend not to give it away. I believe that time is a valuable resource for the spiritual guide and requires some form of compensation for the investment.

Format matters should be carefully and prayerfully considered by the spiritual guide. Each of the various options discussed here hold special opportunities for those seeking help. The effective spiritual guide should seek to present a plan for individuals that is guided by the Holy Spirit, balanced in approach, and holding the best potential for positioning people for the transforming touch of the Lord.

Clarity, Covenants, and Consequences

For over a year I have been part of a mentoring program designed to help pastors grow in Christ. The first phase of the strategy involved selecting twenty qualified pastors who have proven to be particularly effective in ministry. Those chosen embarked upon a year-long relationship experience aimed at equipping them to mentor five other pastors who would be chosen at a later time. A generous grant enabled the seminary to offer this opportunity without cost to all the pastors involved. And as we end this first year everyone agrees that the journey has been a true adventure.

However, the relationship between the first group of pastors and the leadership team was strained a bit as we came close to the end of training. The reason: lack of clarity about specific expectations for the next year. The lead pastors were not complaining about working too hard or having too much responsibility. They rightly wanted to know, as precisely as possible, what was required of them relative to the 100 pastors arriving the following year. That should have been made crystal clear from the very start. No one should be asked to say "yes" to a journey without knowing the destination, required level of involvement, and cost of signing on for the experience. A great deal of anxiety was produced unnecessarily.

The spiritual guide must begin the relationship with absolute *clarity*. The person seeking help should know that the focus of work is upon spiritual maturity, not solving problems. The task of counseling should remain with the counselor. The spiritual guide should discuss that difference with people and feel confident that there is basic understanding and agreement. Other matters, such as time, frequency and length of sessions should be covered and agreed upon. The concept of using activities, exercises and spiritual disciplines as assignments should be reviewed so that there is no misunderstanding. A preliminary discussion of the various options regarding format will also go a long way toward clarifying the nature of spiritual guidance for the seeker. The spiritual guide must also talk about the compensation issue and evaluate if the person seeking help is ready to make the level of commitment needed for the journey.

The spiritual guide should go over these items and then allow the person a week or so to prayerfully consider if he is ready to enter spiritual guidance. Once an individual agrees to move forward, it is time for a *covenant* to be put into place. The spiritual guide should shape this with the individual, including expectations and agreements that are foundational to the relationship. It should detail the commitments to be made by the spiritual guide and the commitments of participation required of the person seeking spiritual guidance. When complete, it should be signed and kept as a covenant, or sacred contract between both parties. Finally it should be sealed in prayer before the Lord.

A covenant is weak unless there are *consequences* for breaking it and once again, this goes both ways. The spiritual guide has the right to expect that the person seeking help will stay engaged in the process, treat them with respect and honor, be honest, and except for emergencies, faithfully attend the sessions ready to work. If these expectations are in any way violated, predetermined consequences can, and in many instances, should be enforced. These are best determined before sessions ever begin and be mutually agreed upon.

The person seeking help should expect that the spiritual guide is faithful to be at the sessions, prepared, attentive and deeply engaged also. The individual has the right to insist upon confidentiality and the proper treatment due a precious child of the Lord. If violated, consequences should be considered, agreed upon prior to beginning spiritual guidance.

I assure you that anyone who has done spiritual direction knows the value of clarity, covenants and consequences. Addressing these issues up front saves a great deal of anxiety along the journey. They serve as solid reminders of what the relationship between spiritual guide and the person being guided is all about. This then enables the Holy Spirit to move both the guide and guided forward into the place of true change, life itself.

Chapter 6

The Landscape of Life

There are two approaches to learning generally employed today. One, which is by far the most common, is the classroom model. Individuals are extracted from their daily context, placed behind a desk and then taught a new vocabulary different from what they normally use. Students are then presented with principles that are said to be highly relevant to the topic at hand and eventually required to test on their ability to remember what was taught. The teacher will emphasize that what is being said is highly important to life, but usually somewhere out in the future. Case studies and examples may be included as a teaching technique, intending that concrete examples will elevate understanding.

This model is often used at seminaries, including the one where I teach. I am required at times to present material this way. This educational approach is certainly better than nothing, but it has serious limitations. Recently I taught several dozen students about how to establish new churches. We sat in a classroom and discussed, for over thirty hours, the intricacies of beginning a church. The topic is important and vital to the Kingdom mission. However, many of the students were not able to completely engage with the subject. Why? Because the topic was not immediately relevant to their life situation. They wanted to learn, but life itself was presenting other demands. Babies were being born, odd jobs were taking time, papers were due for other classes and life was complicated. These students did learn something about church planting, but not with the depth that happens when the topic is relevant to what they are doing at the time.

The second model of learning is much different. It is driven by the immediate need for competency relative to a given life situation. A few days ago the hinge on the door of my daughter's car broke loose. The only way to repair it was to weld it back onto the door. I was motivated to learn, the life situation presented a genuine need and I asked my father for help. He arrived with a welder and carefully taught me how to weld. Involvement in an actual life situation presented a wonderful context for learning and in the end I took the first step toward developing a new skill. The real need drove me to develop a competency that I will use again. The experience of learning went far deeper because I was engaged in life, not a classroom, during the learning opportunity.

Spiritual guidance works best when it is integrated with life, not when it is relegated to the classroom. Imagine a student sitting in a classroom, all the while thinking about the serious fight he had that morning with his spouse. Regardless of the topic, if it is not directly related to that life situation, the student will not be able to fully engage in the moment. Life itself will press into his thinking too much to allow that. Conversely, consider what might happen if that same student happened to be sitting in a lecture that day on conflict in marriage. It is likely that his attention and interest would elevate significantly. The topic would relate to life and as such the teachable moment would be more conducive to learning.

Jesus did not employ a classroom model of spiritual guidance. The Lord understood that the best context for change was life itself, offering wonderful opportunities for personal growth. He stood with His disciples and watched a poor widow place her last bit of money into the temple offering and He turned and spoke to them about sacrifice (Luke 12:1–4). A farmer begins to sow seed in the field and Jesus talks about different types of soil, relating it directly to people's openness to the Kingdom (Matthew 13:1-13). He speaks tenderly about God's concern for the lowly sparrow and then assures people that the Father's love is so much greater for them (Matthew 10:29-31). Jesus demonstrated that life itself was the best context for learning and growth.

One of the best examples of spiritual guidance is found in the gospel of John, chapter 4. Jesus and the disciples travel to Samaria and stop at Sychar near Jacob's well. As the disciples look for food, Jesus rests. A woman arrives who has been beaten down by life. She has a bad reputation in town and goes to the well when no one else is there in order to avoid ridicule. Married five times, she is presently living with a man who is not her husband. Her life is barren in every sense of that word. The Samaritan woman brought far more than a jug to the well that day. She carried in her heart all the pain of a broken life.

Jesus, seeing her emptiness, begins a conversation by asking for a drink of water. That simple request opens the door to a discussion about prejudice, worship, living water, broken relationships and eventually eternal life. The woman is lovingly confronted with her own spiritual poverty. And what is most important is her response to this particular moment in her life. The Samaritan woman could have been resentful and willfully turned away from Jesus and gone back to her life. But instead, she responds to Christ and is changed by the encounter.

Life itself, in all its brokenness and pain, was the context for spiritual direction in Jesus' ministry. He met people right were their lives were most complex and offered them another way, a different path, an opportunity for change. The people who stepped into the guidance of Christ were transformed radically. Their names are now synonymous with sainthood, but their first encounters with Christ were earthed in very broken situations. Zacchaeus, Mary Magdalene, the Gadarene demoniac, the woman caught in adultery, Simon Peter, Matthew, and countless other people of the New Testament

Church were helped by Christ to choose the path that led to new life. They responded to the spiritual guidance of the Lord and the choice they made positioned them for the transforming work of the Holy Spirit. That is spiritual guidance at its very best.

The "All Things" Plan of God

The concept of God's "all things" plan was presented previously, but it would serve this discussion to briefly revisit it. Romans 8:29 reveals that the Father's plan, from the foundation of the earth, is to transform people into the image of His Son, Jesus. The verse preceding speaks of God causing *"all things* [to] *work together for good to those who love God, who have been called according to his purpose."* This means that God is in fact willing to use all things to shape His people into the likeness of the Lord Jesus Christ. That includes the good and the bad, the positive and the negative, successes and failures, joys and sorrows – all things.

It is essential, however, that people respond to life events in ways that give the Lord permission to use such challenges for His greater purpose. When they do, the Lord releases the Spirit to bring life. When people do not respond well, allowing bitterness and anger to take over, they experience even deeper levels of brokenness. Take Kevin for example. He was unjustly released from his job, which created great hardship for his family. Kevin was justifiably upset and had to deal before the Lord with serious anger and resentment. But, with the help of a spiritual guide, he was able to meet God in new ways through the unfortunate event. It was a difficult struggle, but Kevin positioned himself before the Lord and asked that the dismissal be used of God to change him. The Lord met him in that prayer.

Amy, Kevin's wife, responded much differently. She too was hurt by what happened and rightly so. But rather than deal with the pain before the Lord, she grew bitter and resentful, eventually blaming Kevin's employers, Kevin, and ultimately

God. She desperately grappled for control and allowed her anger to take over. Stuck in her need for justice and refusing to forgive, Amy has lost ground in her Christian walk. Two people, the same situation, opposite responses, which led to very different places.

There are four important principles related to the "all things" plan of God.

▶ *Principle 1:*
How people respond to life's challenges shapes them more than the events themselves.

It is impossible to deny this principle, for it is proven every single day. Life is certainly tough and filled with unexpected trials. Many times the events that come one's way threaten people at the deepest level of existence. But what matters in the long run is how a person responds to what has happened. More times than I can remember I have watched as two people face the same challenge in life and yet respond in different ways. The event hits each person with the same force, but the response each made set them on a course for a very different destination. The previous example of Kevin and Amy makes that point clearly.

▶ *Principle 2:*
God is present in every moment of life, ready to bring change to those who surrender to His purposes.

I want to be clear that I am not suggesting that God is the cause of all the difficulties and trials that life affords. Living in a fallen world, the presence of evil and poor personal choices have a great deal to do with the tough times people face. But this truth I do know. God is present in every moment and willing to meet people right in the midst of the darkness.

Years ago a Jesuit priest named Jean-Pierre de Caussade was assigned the responsibility of serving as spiritual guide for a group of nuns. Much of his guidance is contained in the book, *The Sacrament of the Present Moment.* There he writes,

"You are seeking God, dear sister, and he is everywhere. Everything proclaims him to you, everything reveals him to you, everything brings him to you. He is by your side, over you, around you, within you ... you seek perfection and it lies in everything that happens to you – your suffering, your actions, your impulses are the mysteries under which God reveals himself to you."[8]

This principle is foundational to spiritual direction. Regardless of what life affords, God is present to help the believer. If an individual is guided to respond appropriately, events that were intent on breaking them, will actually be used of the Lord to draw them into Christ-likeness. That does not mean that such challenges are fair, or easy to handle. Nor does it mean that individual does not need to vent before the Lord. But deep beneath the pain is the presence of God. The spiritual guide must know how to help someone go there and experience deep change.

▶ *Principle 3:*
The spiritual guide must help people develop spiritual sensitivity in order to respond to God's presence in life.
In the poem "Aurora Leigh", Elizabeth Barrett Browning wrote,

> "Earth's crammed with heaven,
> Every common bush afire with God;
> But only he who sees takes off his shoes;
> The rest sit round it and pick blackberries."

While all of creation is alive with the presence of God, most people miss Him. They have not developed their spiritual senses and have difficulty seeing and sensing the movement of the Lord in life. While individuals complain that God is

---

[8]   De Caussade, Jean-Pierre, *The Sacrament of the Present Moment* (New York, New York: HarperCollins, 1989), p. 18.

distant and silent, the real problem lies with people. They do not have "eyes that see and ears that hear."

If people are going to respond to the "all things" plan of God, they must be able to recognize His movement in the challenges that come their way. One of the most important responsibilities of the spiritual guide is helping people with this process. The spiritual guide should encourage those seeking help to practice the presence of God, growing in attentiveness to His voice and leading. It is essential to responding to God in the sacrament of the present moment. In the following chapter a number of spiritual exercises and spiritual disciplines will be discussed in detail. The spiritual guide must integrate these practices into sessions and assignments. They are designed to open people to the presence and movement of the Holy Spirit, by developing the spiritual sensitivities of the seeker. Spiritual awareness is foundational to respond properly to the challenges life brings.

▶ *Principle 4:*
With the "all things" plan of God, surrender is the pathway to change and personal growth.
Surrendering to life does not mean, "Go ahead Life, do whatever you want." Surrender is an obedient response to God in the midst of difficult circumstances. There are several forces behind what happens to people and each have a selfish agenda. The evil one wants to see people destroyed, sinful people want to use others for their purposes, the self-seeking individual wants to see either pleasure or power result from what happens to them. But the Christian is called to surrender to only one agenda, "whatever the Father desires." The prayer of the surrendered is, "Lord use this to your glory, transforming me into the likeness of your Son, Jesus Christ."

The prayer of surrender is far from easy to offer to the Lord. Many times the events of life are very hard, deeply painful and long in duration. It is quite natural for anyone to want to grab control and fix matters. But the spiritual guide should sensitively and caringly help people open their hands and offer what has happened to the Lord as a vehicle of change. The spiritual guide will need to be patient, offer needed support and never minimize the difficulty of such a stance. The spiritual guide will need to invite people to speak out frustrations and complaints before the Lord as a personal lament. But in time, the spiritual guide will point to the "all things" plan and encourage surrender. It is the greatest gift a believer can offer the Lord, for it is grounded in a deep trust in the Father's unconditional love.

Engaging Life through Spiritual Guidance

As previously stated, life affords the best opportunity for an individual's growth toward Christ-likeness. It is important that the spiritual guide sees the events of life as the context for instruction, illustration, engagement of spiritual sensitivities and the transforming work of the Holy Spirit. Learning to do this will certainly take time. But the more a spiritual guide serves people on the journey toward Christ, the more comfortable and skilled she will be with the process. What follows is an example of spiritual guidance that integrates fundamental principles faithful to understanding life events as the context for personal change.

Garry Lawson was one of the most promising students to attend the seminary. He was bright, friendly, hungry for Christ and excited about serving the Lord. I was able to spend time with Garry and three other students every other week for spiritual direction. We allowed life to set the agenda and each grew closer to one another and closer to the Lord. At graduation, Garry was appointed to a mid-size congregation as pastor, which excited him and his wife Carla. He had worked hard for three years preparing for ministry and now had the opportunity to help others grow in Christ.

As with all pastorates, there were ups and downs with Garry's experience at the church. Many people loved him. But there was a handful of the old guard who were neither kind nor patient with him. They continually let Garry know where he fell short in their eyes and made most meetings unpleasant for everyone present. At first Garry weathered the storms well, trusting the Lord and giving his all. But one event challenged that, leading Garry to question whether he could continue as their pastor.

The church had agreed to reimburse Garry for travel expenses related to ministry, which is to be expected. But at one meeting a member of this group who opposed Garry accused him of stealing that money. Garry was stunned and asked for clarification. The complaining member said that he had records that Garry had submitted expenses for taking youth to a basketball game and going out to dinner with another couple.

This man, backed by his group of malcontents, proceeded to say that Garry was not permitted to use that money for such things and was in fact stealing. Even though Garry explained that he was doing ministry, they were not satisfied, saying he got personal pleasure out of such things and was using the funds in an unethical way. Garry was devastated. Even though the majority of the people at the meeting supported Garry in this matter, he was deeply hurt and wanted to leave the congregation immediately. He called and asked me for time, which I was more than happy to give.

Before the session I spent time before the Lord, asking for help. I wanted to serve Jesus and Garry the very best I could, under the Spirit's guidance. I prepared the office, setting an atmosphere that was quiet and restful, playing soft music and lighting a candle. When Garry arrived I greeted him with honest joy and embraced my hurting friend.

Within moments I asked Garry to take a seat and I waited upon the Lord in prayer. I spent time in quiet and then invited the Holy Spirit to be present with us in the moment. I encouraged Garry to pray aloud, explaining to the Lord why he had come. Before closing the time of prayer, I led Garry in a prayer exercise designed to help him find a safe place within himself, where he could center upon the Lord and listen to His voice. This took several moments, but very soon Garry was in that place. After a brief time of silence, we concluded that time of prayer. This exercise will be discussed in detail in the next chapter.

I asked Garry to share about the event that led him into this session. I wanted him to feel free to say everything about what had occurred down to the smallest detail, as long as it was important to him. I listened, asked the occasional question that would help keep Garry focused and gave him room to vent as much as he needed. I did not censor or try to get him to state anything in a different way. I made no suggestions and offered no advice. I was simply there, listening.

The first step I took toward direction focused on the feeling level. I asked Garry specific questions about his emotional response to what took place. I asked him to link feelings to specific moments and events in the meeting. I believe that feelings tell the spiritual director a great deal about how a person is processing a life event. He said that he was shocked at the accusation, frustrated that those people were being unreasonable, and angry. He repeated it again saying that he was very angry and wanted to quit right there and then. Garry told me that he wanted to go across the room and grab the man and hurt him. Understandably.

The time had come for the session to end. I instructed Garry to spend some time before the next session writing a psalm of lament to the Lord about what happened. I wanted him to be honest with the Lord, not censoring what he was writing to make it sound spiritual. Most important to the lament would be Garry's feelings and beliefs that related to the church conflict. There was no suggestion whatsoever that we try to resolve the tension. That was not part of this spiritual guidance. Because Garry was struggling deeply, we agreed to meet again the next week. After committing each other into the hands of the Lord, we parted.

The next week I prepared for Garry's coming as I had done many times previously. My prayer focused upon the Lord's will for the session and I felt sure the time had come to move

Garry to the next step in guidance. After greeting each other we again spent time silently opening ourselves to the ministry of the Holy Spirit. I asked Garry, while still in the attitude of prayer, to read his lament before the Father, assuring him of my support and presence. The time was powerful as Garry spoke emotionally about embarrassment, shame, feelings of rejection and deep anger. As he focused upon the event, Garry was honest about believing that he was all alone, unappreciated by many people and finished there as a pastor. I did not try to reframe anything Garry said. Right or wrong, true or false, what he said was honestly what he believed and how Garry felt. The moment was sacred and Garry had a real sense that the Father had heard his cry.

The Holy Spirit confirmed that we should move to the next step before ending that session. I asked Garry to begin considering where the Lord was in all of this. Specifically, I wanted Garry to ask the Lord two questions. "How did the Father feel about what happened to him?" and "What was God desiring to do in Garry's life through this event?" Garry discussed possibilities briefly and then our time came to a close. I asked Garry to do three things each day. First, he was to go to his safe place in prayer and experience the presence of the Father. Second, he was to ask the Father to open his spiritual senses. Third, he was to present the two questions to the Lord and be attentive for an answer.

The week seemed to pass quickly and before I knew it Garry and I were once again before the Lord. He came in ready to work and told me about his experiences in prayer. Garry talked about personal resistance, interruptions and even some avoidance. These are normal struggles for any person seeking the Lord. But he also told me that he eventually thought he heard from the Father, but was not all that sure. Such hesitation is understandable. It is easy to project one's own feelings into the moment, putting our words into God's mouth. While the Spirit of Christ is certainly within each believer, no one should assume that everything they hear comes straight from Him. And so we both committed to lay everything we sensed and heard before the Holy Spirit and the Word.

Garry told me that he thought that the Lord had said that He deeply loved him. While this word seemed certainly obvious from Scripture, it touched Garry deeply, especially in this situation. He was struggling with great anger and had thoughts that were certainly not Christ-like. Yet, the second part of the message was much more challenging. Garry sensed the Lord asking him a question: "Will you allow Me to love this man through you, Garry?" When I asked Garry how he felt about all this, he was honest. He did not want to show that man love. He wanted him to pay for what he did, or at the very least tell everyone at the church that he was wrong in the way he treated Garry. Reaching out in the love of Christ was the last thing Garry wanted to do.

The assignment for this next week was clear. Garry was to be attentive to the tension between what he wanted and what the Lord was asking of him. Specifically, I wanted Garry to become conscious of his internal struggle, identifying by the Spirit's help his own barriers and resistance to surrendering to God's work. The exercise I sent him away with was to repeat the "Jesus Prayer" throughout each day. Garry left the session feeling far more conflict than when he arrived. That was good. It was evidence that he was deeply engaged in the process.

As Garry arrived for the following session I had the Eucharist prepared for us to celebrate. We read the story of the Lord's Supper in John chapter 13, including the account of Jesus washing the disciple's feet. It was a special time at the table of the Lord. After receiving the elements I asked Garry about what he learned this week. He quickly responded, "I am not Jesus." I asked him to explain his remark and he told me that it was not in his heart to be nice to this obnoxious man. But then he remarked, "But I need to be." At that moment I knew that Garry did not need my help any longer. He was positioned for a work that only the Holy Spirit could accomplish. He was willing and he was surrendered.

In truth the spiritual guide does not need to say a great deal when helping others. In this case, the entire guidance revolved around seven basic questions:

- *What happened?*
- *How did you feel about what happened?*
- *What did you believe about God, yourself, and others relative to what happened?*
- *How does God feel about what happened to you?*
- *What does God want to do in your life through this?*
- *How are you responding to God?*
- *How should you respond?*

Wrapped around these questions are time, conversation, prayer, spiritual exercises and specific assignments, all directed to opening a person up to the movement of God through a life event. Under the guidance of the Holy Spirit, this process positions a person for deep and lasting change. The problem of the life event may yet need to be resolved, but that is not the work of the spiritual guide. This ministry is about developing spiritual sensitivities in people so that they can be positioned for the transforming touch of the Lord.

Suffering and Spiritual Guidance

I do not believe that all suffering is part of God's will for people. It is more often than not the devastating consequence of living in a fallen world that is infested with evil spirits and populated with sinful people. The pain and heartache that many people across the world experience is not part of a divine plan that demands human suffering. Starving infants, dying mothers and the ravages of AIDS in Africa today does not bring God pleasure. Suffering is not a part of Christ's prayer, *"Your kingdom come, your will be done on earth as it is in heaven"* (Matthew 6:10). The Kingdom of heaven is free from suffering and the presence of suffering here is a daily reminder that we are not yet home.

Having said that, I do believe two things about suffering that are foundational to offering life events as a context for change. First, Jesus enters personal suffering through the incarnation. He walked this earth and felt the full weight of the fall, including getting an up-close look at human misery. And Christ consistently healed the broken and set them free. He never told people to accept suffering as God's will. Christ reached out to those in pain and touched them deeply. Jesus, as Nouwen reminds us, "enters our sadness, takes us by the hand, pulls us up gently and invites us to dance . . . because at the center of our grief we find the grace of God."[9] The spiritual guide should help the hurting to experience the presence of Jesus in the place of great pain. It will not be easy, but it is a vital part of providing spiritual guidance. Many who have met Jesus in suffering discover a depth of intimacy with God they never before dreamed possible. That is His gift to the broken.

Secondly, when offered to God, suffering can be used of the Lord to transform a person into the likeness of Christ. It certainly is not an easy path and such a step requires willingness and surrender. But the testimony of the ages is that the likeness of Christ is often shaped through deep loss and pain. It is an irony for sure, yet many who have gone before point the way. By some miraculous act of love, the Father can redeem suffering in a person's life, leaving newness where death and destruction once sought to do their work. This takes a tremendous act of trust, but when extended heavenward, that trust brings transforming power.

The spiritual guide must move sensitively when suffering is part of the journey for a person. The hurting individual needs to be encouraged to speak honestly about pain and loss before the Lord, without the spiritual guide feeling the need to reframe what is being said. The spiritual guide must refrain from spewing out devastating spiritual clichés that do great

---

[9] Nouwen, Henri, *Turn My Mourning into Dancing: Moving Through Hard Times with Hope* (Nashville, Tennessee: W Publishing Group, 2001), p. 13.

damage to the hurting. The spiritual guide must patiently walk the hurting to the Lord for an honest conversation. And the spiritual guide should wait patiently, giving the Holy Spirit room to work. In time the hurting person will meet the Suffering Servant and movement will begin. Spiritual disciplines and spiritual exercises can be an important part of positioning people for that encounter. Attention will be given to these essential resources of spiritual development in the following chapter.

Chapter 7

Tools and Skills
for Spiritual Guidance

I played intercollegiate soccer for fours years during my undergraduate days at Geneva College. I was not necessarily a stand out athlete, but I thoroughly enjoyed the camaraderie and competition of sport. Each summer I looked forward to arriving on campus two weeks before classes began to begin preparation for the upcoming fall season. The coach would hold tryouts and those making the team were then required to undergo the most demanding schedule of daily practice, which included endless laps around the field, grueling calisthenics and the constant repetition of drills aimed at developing very specific skills related to the game of soccer. In many ways the practices were hard, boring and long. But no one ever saw a moment of playing time without the dedication and discipline of daily workouts.

I have often thought about the relationship between "practice" and the "game". Each week the team would work out for a minimum of fifteen hours in preparation for a match. It was not unusual to repeat one particular skill hour upon hour, in anticipation that that move might be needed as part of a winning strategy. The game itself lasted a mere ninety minutes and some of the skills we rehearsed were required for a moment that was only seconds long. Yet the ability to execute that particular maneuver meant the difference between victory and defeat. Many times the people in the stands celebrated the skill a player demonstrated as he made a particular play and attributed it to natural ability and gifting. But the truth was that even the best players had practiced long hours anticipating that one moment of opportunity. Excellence on the athletic field takes discipline and focused training for every athlete. Some people are certainly more agile, fast, or coordinated than others. But even the Michael Jordon's of the world need lots of practice before the game begins.

The Christian life also demands discipline and training in preparation for what life brings. The follower of Christ cannot expect to respond properly to challenges in the moment of trial without carefully developing appropriate spiritual sensitivities through daily devotion to the Lord. The person who waits until the storm hits with full force before learning to pray may have waited far too long. Those who never took the time to recognize the voice of God in daily life will seldom hear Him speak when the noise of life is at its loudest. Individuals who were too busy to practice the presence of God when days were full of light will be lost when the darkness of evil suddenly sets in upon them.

In some ways the spiritual guide is like a coach. He lovingly, yet boldly requires that the person seeking help spends time developing his spiritual senses. These senses are essential to finding God in the moments of life and foundational to responding in ways that welcome the transforming work of the Holy Spirit. The spiritual guide prayerfully selects disciplines and exercises, historically proven to develop spiritual maturity and assigns them strategically. The purpose for such disciplines and exercises is always clearly defined and specifically focused. Spiritual disciplines and spiritual exercises position an individual for God's presence each day, developing a deeper, more intimate relationship with Him. They also equip a believer with the "eyes to see and ears to hear" when life is far more complicated and threatening.

Spiritual Disciplines

There are more than a few Christians who immediately draw back at the mention of spiritual disciplines. Frankly, I understand the way they feel. There was a time when my reaction was, "Oh no, not another talk about having a devotional life." My workaholic past had soured me on "devotions." I saw spiritual disciplines as another hoop I had to jump through to be a good Christian. I was tired and frustrated and already felt guilty about my relationship with the Lord. The thought of adding spiritual disciplines to my life only increased my anxiety. The effective spiritual guide must be prepared to address people's negative feelings, helping them see that spiritual disciplines, far from being hard and boring, position people for incredible moments in the Lord's loving presence.

Spiritual disciplines should be explained to people as activities that help them experience God's presence and develop their spiritual senses. They do not, in themselves, change people's lives. Instead, spiritual disciplines, when properly embraced, position individuals to encounter God, which is in fact the foundation of all transformation. This difference may seem subtle, but it is a significant redefinition of the purpose and power of spiritual disciplines. People who strive to make things happen through spiritual disciplines are caught in a frustrating trap of works-righteousness which requires the power of the flesh. But those who embrace spiritual disciplines as doorways to God's touch do so in joyful anticipation that the Holy Spirit may move through such activities to change their lives. It is an open-handed, surrendered heart approach to the devotional life.

Spiritual disciplines are channels of grace that complement the journey to Christ-likeness. They are activities that, in their very nature, reflect the character of Jesus Christ and follow the example of His ministry. Jesus practiced spiritual disciplines and as such so should every follower of Christ. The spiritual guide should practice spiritual disciplines as part of his own journey to Jesus. Doing this will lend integrity and experience to the spiritual guidance relative to this topic.

In recent years there have been several very helpful books on spiritual disciplines. Probably the best-known work is Richard Foster's *Celebration of Discipline*. He provides a thorough and practical discussion of the nature and practice of each particular spiritual discipline. I also appreciate Dallas Willard's work, *The Spirit of the Disciplines*. I especially find his two categories of disciplines valuable when offering spiritual guidance. Willard places each spiritual discipline under one of two separate headings; the Disciplines of Abstinence and the Disciplines of Engagement.

The Disciplines of Abstinence include:

- *Solitude*: Choosing to come apart from daily activity in order to be alone with God.
- *Silence*: Choosing to step away from the noise of the world in order to listen to the whispers of God.
- *Fasting*: Abstaining from food for a specific period of time in order to lessen the grip of the flesh, opening the way to God's strength in weakness.
- *Frugality*: In a world of material excess, choosing to say "no" to luxuries and wants, focusing upon God as the satisfaction of all life.
- *Chastity*: Choosing to set aside, for a season, the sexual aspect of the marriage relationship in order to concentrate on spiritual union. An abstinence in marriage demands mutual consent.
- *Secrecy*: Consciously choosing to follow the admonition of Jesus and do deeds of service and giving in private.
- *Sacrifice*: Giving beyond one's ability in response to God's self-giving.

The Disciplines of Engagement include:

- *Study*: Choosing to spend time meditating upon Scripture. The goal of this discipline is not acquiring information, but instead experiencing God in the Word.

- **Worship**: Declaring the wonder and supreme worth of God, engaging heart, mind, soul and body in an ongoing offering of adoration.
- **Celebration**: Choosing to find and experience joy in the life God gives, celebrating the goodness of the created order in all its beauty and greatness.
- **Service**: Engaging resources, talents and spiritual gifts in ministry to others, accepting Jesus' example of servant-hood through the towel and basin.
- **Prayer**: Through the power of the Holy Spirit, communing with God through prayer, as well as affecting the world and the spiritual realm through requests and petitions.
- **Fellowship**: Choosing to actively integrate into the healthy, spiritual community as a place of united strength, increased faith and demonstrated love.
- **Confession**: Jesus works through weakness and brings wholeness as people bring all things into the light. This discipline involves opening broken hearts before one another for mutual strength and support.
- **Submission**: Choosing to come under the authority and direction of those in anointed spiritual leadership.

How should the spiritual director help people select the disciplines to be embraced and developed? I suggest that there are two factors that will guide most decisions. First, the spiritual guide should help people engage in the spiritual disciplines that most directly address the areas of weakness in their lives. Most people have some aspects of spiritual sensitivity more developed than others. One person seeking help might struggle with greed and power, and as such should be assigned the disciplines of sacrifice, secrecy, service and submission. If lust of the flesh is controlling a person's life, fasting, confession and submission would be a good place to begin. The spiritual director's choice of disciplines should specifically address issues that God seems to be identifying in the person's walk toward Christ-likeness.

A second consideration is most certainly prayer and the guidance of the Holy Spirit. I believe that the Holy Spirit will lay specific disciplines upon the heart of the spiritual guide or the person seeking help. These disciplines should be especially practiced, given the basic philosophy that a faithful disciple wants to obey the leading of the Lord. I often sense the Lord drawing me to specific disciplines. At times the reason seems obvious, and yet at other times initially less clear. But eventually I always see that the Lord was leading me to specific disciplines in order to develop a much needed part of my relationship with Him.

Accountability is an important aspect of assigning spiritual disciplines to an individual. The spiritual guide should explain the purpose of embracing such activities and give individuals general guidelines about how to best engage them into the rhythms of life. I use the following questions in sessions that are scheduled after a person begins to include spiritual disciplines as part of the journey.

- *What feelings did you have as you moved toward the spiritual discipline?*
- *What, if any, resistance did you experience?*
- *Were you able to sense the presence of the Lord?*
- *If so, how did you respond?*
- *If not, what did you feel?*
- *What is happening now that you have embraced this discipline?*
- *How can I best support you as you move forward in this activity?*

There are many rich and wonderful insights to be gained by the spiritual guide related to the practice of spiritual disciplines. Each and every activity is multi-dimensional, able by God's power to deeply impact a person's life and journey to Christ-likeness. Learning more about spiritual disciplines will enhance a person's ministry of spiritual guidance, helping the spiritual guide serve people in ways that truly make a Kingdom difference in their lives.

Spiritual Exercises

I must confess that as a protestant Christian, the concept of spiritual exercises was foreign to me. I mistakenly believed that such activities were part of an unhealthy mysticism void of balance and spiritual depth. In the circles where I served the Lord and experienced the Christian life, I had more than a few fellow unbelievers. But when the dark night of the soul descended and all my normal ways of responding to life failed, the writings of the Christian mystics helped me find my way home again. I stumbled upon the literature of Fenelon, Guyon, Molinos and Brother Lawrence. It became clear that they knew the path to life and so I took the risk and chose to follow. Along the way I discovered century-old spiritual exercises that quietly, yet powerfully brought under-standing and life back into my lost, weary soul. The savage events of life demanded that I deepen my relationship with Christ. I willingly embraced vehicles of His grace that before I had rejected outright. Pride was gone and pure desperation took over. I have never been the same and the practices of the saints have become lights along the journey for me.

All of life can be a sacrament of grace if a person allows. God is not only present in every moment, but aspects of His touch are found in all that He has made. It is as Richard Rohr says, a "sacramental universe." But to experience God in all of life, a person must receive guidance and help. Spiritual senses need to be developed, which is part of the spiritual guide's work in helping others journey to Christ. Spiritual exercises are intended to be instruments of that process, opening the spiritual sight, hearing, taste, touch and smell of the pilgrim, so that regardless of light or dark, day or night, he can perceive the movement of God in life.

I teach a class on spiritual guidance to doctoral students. There is one assignment that I give that illustrates the central point of this discussion. I require that each student bring a magnifying glass to class. I spend some time instructing them on the concept of transposition, the fact that God has placed aspects of His own presence and power in all that He has created. I then ask each student to prayerfully seek the Holy Spirit's help as they go outside and discover the wonder of God through the magnifying glass. I ask them to move slowly, patiently, and allow the Lord to speak to them personally through this exercise. I am always overjoyed as students return so excited about what they experienced. Invariably the Lord whispers a very personal message to each person in a way he or she had never considered previously. Suddenly their senses open to the possibility that all of life could be a sacrament of grace, a means of experiencing the Father of all creation.

There are countless spiritual exercises that hold potential for spiritual growth. I am limiting this discussion to seven:

- *the safe place*
- *simple prayer*
- *Scripture*
- *stillness*
- *solitude*
- *symbols*
- *sacrament.*

The spiritual guide should approach spiritual exercises as he does with other matters related to spiritual guidance. Activities should be assigned at the leading of the Holy Spirit and selected because each is useful to specific aspects of spiritual development. The spiritual guide must emphasize that the power does not rest within the spiritual exercises themselves. They serve merely as another way to position a person before the Lord. The attitude of the individual and the welcome of the Holy Spirit matter most. But those who are open will find that the Lord honors the surrender of a willing heart.

The safe place

Most people come for spiritual guidance in noticeable emotional pain. The challenges of life and the insensitive people in their world have intensified the deep sense that life involves a great deal of risk and at times significant hurt. The wounded who come are more often than not trying to protect themselves from further injury. They work hard to keep themselves safe and tend to be untrusting, even with the Lord. While they may be pleasant and engaging, the wounded have constructed a complex system of defense to guard against further harm. The defenses themselves are often doing far more damage than good and invariably keep even those who could help at a distance. Whether it is intended or not, the walls people build to keep others away also block access to the Father and His healing power.

The safe place exercise is designed to help people open up to the Lord and enable them to spend time communing and healing in the light of His presence. It is a spiritual exercise of guided imagery based upon theological truths found in the Bible. The spiritual guide must make it clear that opening the imagination to the Holy Spirit's touch is simply another way to embrace what God says to be true in His word. For example, Psalm 121 teaches that God watches over His own, even as they sleep. Many people can understand what that text is saying, yet the truth of God's faithful watch-care does not penetrate into the places of deep hurt. Through Spirit-led guided imagery, the person allows his sanctified imagination to create a picture of that reality and then rests there in safety with the Lord.

The following steps will serve as a guide to this activity.

- *Step 1*: Get into a comfortable position, relax your body and open yourself to the presence of the Holy Spirit. It is often helpful to light a candle and put on soft, inspirational music. Be patient and still.
- *Step 2*: Begin to breath in slowly and deeply, inviting the Holy Spirit to fill you with His presence and sanctify your imagination.
- *Step 3*: Ask the Holy Spirit to create a picture in your imagination of a safe place. It might be a place you fondly

remember, or a special spot along a stream, or mountain-side, or beach.

- **Step 4**: As you relax there, invite Jesus to enter your safe place. Open your spiritual senses to the light and warmth that He brings.
- **Step 5**: Begin to sense the love that radiates from Christ. Feel it filling you and bringing you great rest and peace. You are His beloved and He longs to be with you.
- **Step 6**: Choose one word or phrase that sums up your response to Christ. Begin to say it over and again as an offering of your love.
- **Step 7**: Relax in this special place, allowing your heart to fill with Christ. Rest in His presence. Rest in His love. You were created for this intimate embrace. Be safe there.
- **Step 8**: Give thanks to the Lord for His presence. Amen.

The spiritual guide would do well to introduce the safe place exercise soon into the relationship. It could take some time for people to experience the Holy Spirit's touch in this way. If there are barriers and resistance the effective spiritual guide will use that as a context for discussion and growth. I have had some people find this difficult to do, so I ask them to draw what they wish their safe place were like and then imagine being there with the Lord. The primary goal is to help individuals find a place, deep within themselves, where they feel safe and can rest in the arms of Jesus.

Simple prayer

Most people find prayer intimidating. They mistakenly have the notion that to be acceptable before the Lord, prayers must be said in just the right way, with just the right words. Some see prayer as a spiritual art reserved for the gifted and holy. But the truth is that Jesus was not impressed with long rambling prayers that have the appearance of spiritual maturity, but are in fact self-serving and empty (Matthew 6:5–13). He encouraged His followers to practice a more simple form of prayer, following a general guideline that when the heart is right before the Father, less is really more.

The prayers of Jesus were often quite brief. When in Gethsemane He simply said, *"Abba, Father ... everything is possible for you. Take this cup from me. Yet not what I will, but what you will"* (Mark 14:36). His three prayers from the cross, at a time of tremendous agony and need, were equally short, directly to the point and filled with emotion: *"Father forgive them, for they do not know what they are doing"* (Luke 23:34); *"My God, my God, why have you forsaken me"* (Mark 15:34), and, *"Father, into your hands I commit my spirit"* (Luke 23:46). The Lord did not ramble on and on, but instead allowed the cry of His heart to flow out in honest words directed to the Father of love.

Prayer is far more a state of the heart than state of the art. The spiritual guide should help people practice simple prayer. For centuries believers all over the world have embraced the *Jesus Prayer* as a way of making their requests be made known to the Lord. The *Jesus Prayer*, as it is now called, comes from the cry of a blind beggar who was at the side of the road as Jesus was passing by (Luke 18:35–43). Upon discovering that the Lord was near, the blind beggar called out, *"Jesus, Son of David, have mercy on me!"* (Luke 18:38). People tried to silence the man, telling him to be quiet, *"but he shouted all the more, 'Jesus, Son of David, have mercy on me!' "* (Luke 18:39). The Lord Jesus was deeply moved by the man's cry, complimented him on his faith, and healed him of blindness.

To the hurting and lost, the words, *"Jesus, Son of David, have mercy on me!"* are packed with meaning. It is as if all the needs of a needy individual are contained in those eight words. The spiritual guide should prayerfully introduce the *Jesus Prayer* to people, asking that they repeat it often through the day. I instruct individuals to picture every personal need entering those eight words. I tell them that every time they honestly lift up that simple prayer, they are actually surrendering all things before the mercy of the Lord. I encourage people to pray the *Jesus Prayer* many times a day, allowing it to draw them toward the One who hears and cares.

Another form of simple prayer is called the *breath prayer*. This format of prayer was developed by Ron DelBene, and discussed in his book *The Breath of Life: A Simple Way to Pray*. The *breath prayer* constitutes a person's deepest heart cry. It is normally only a short phrase or sentence that best expresses an individual's spiritual hunger and when it is prayed, opens the heart to a new attentiveness and awareness of the Father's love. Discovering one's *breath prayer* occurs through a simple visualization exercise. A person is to sit quietly before the Lord, opening themselves to the presence of the Holy Spirit. They are then to imagine the Lord standing with arms extended, calling the person by name and asking, "[Name], what do you want?" DelBene recommends that the believer allows the answer to come from the deepest place within the heart. That cry, contained in a few words becomes a *breath prayer*. The spiritual guide would do well to use this spiritual exercise, encouraging people to breathe that prayer each moment of the day. It will open the seeker to a new encounter with God's presence and transforming love.

Scripture

The spiritual guide should help people turn to Scripture in ways that actually enable them to encounter the power of the living Word. Once again, spiritual senses must be developed to fully appreciate the movement of the Holy Spirit through Scripture. Two specific spiritual exercises, both centuries old, can serve the spiritual guide well to this end; *lectio divina* and *the four-stranded garland*.

Lectio divina is actually an ancient approach to Scripture that was widely practiced in the church. It involves a very slow reading or listening to the Word, married to a form of contemplative prayer that, together, opens the reader to the presence of God. *Lectio divina* has four movements. First, the reader, or listener, turns to a selected passage of Scripture with a sense of humility and deep awe, listening for the whisper of God spoken personally, intimately to the reader. The key to this movement is allowing the word to be alive for this moment, in this day. That is called the *lectio*, or listening phase. Next, the reader begins to ponder all the implications of the scripture as it relates to the personal Word from God. This involves allowing the scripture to interact with the reader's feelings, thoughts, hopes and concerns. Time is taken to repeat the fresh word from God, meditating on its implications for life. This is called *meditatio*, or *meditation*.

Next the reader moves into a form of prayer that is far more dialogue than monologue. The reader begins a loving, intimate conversation with the Father. The goal is to embrace the word into the deepest place within the heart allowing it to bring change to the true self. This phase is known as *oratio*, or *prayer*. Finally, the reader rests before God. Little is spoken, but much is communicated between the reader and the Father. Willingness and surrender to the message of the word have brought peace. This is known as *contemplatio*, or *contemplation*.

The spiritual guide should select appropriate, brief passages that relate to the movement of God in the person's life. These should be the focal point of *lectio divina* within the sessions, as the spiritual guide introduces the practice. Eventually assignments should be given that take this spiritual discipline beyond the time together and into daily life. It is vital that the spiritual guide processes what has happened during *lectio divina*.

A second and personal favorite among scriptural exercises is known as *the four-stranded garland*. History tells us that Martin Luther was asked by his barber for help in understanding Scripture. Luther provided him with a simple four-step approach to God's Word that has become known as *the four-stranded garland*. Essentially the reader is to take a small passage of Scripture and move prayerfully through the following steps. First, read the text with an open heart, looking for a specific instruction that the Lord has given. Next, the reader is to give thanks for all the possibilities that God has given through this text. Third, the reader is to ask the Holy Spirit to enlighten their heart to any sin that needs to be confessed related to the passage. Finally, the person is to look for practical ways to respond to this scripture. I use this practice regularly and published a devotional guide built upon *the four-stranded garland,* entitled *A More Excellent Way.* The practice is an invaluable spiritual exercise and should be prayerfully used as part of spiritual guidance.

Stillness

Stillness is the close companion of Scripture. In a world filled with noise, the spiritual exercise of stillness re-centers a person, opening a deep awareness of the true self and of God's presence. Henri Nouwen wrote:

> "The word of God draws us into silence; silence makes us attentive to God's work. The word of God penetrates though the thick of human verbosity to the silent center of our heart; silence opens in us a space where the word can be heard." [10]

Every Christian needs a deep inner space where the word can be heard. If the spiritual guide is going to help people listen for the whispers of God, they must assign the spiritual exercise of silence. It is the only way to reject the maddening cacophony of sound that shuts out the word that truly sets people free. Silence alone stills the storm of noise that leads to so much internal unrest. Anselm Gruen writes:

> "In silence the inner disturbances can quiet down, the dust cloud can settle, to let the heart clear up. It is like cloudy wine, which becomes clear after lying quietly in storage." [11]

How desperately people today need that rest, the quiet of green pasture and still water. The Word of God commands

---

[10] Nouwen, Henri, *Reaching Out: The Three Movements of Life* (New York, New York: Image Books, 1975).

[11] Gruen, Anselm, *Heaven Begins within You: Wisdom from the Desert Fathers* (New York, New York: Crossroads Publishing Company, 1999), p. 58.

stillness and believers today would find life if they would obey (Psalm 46:10).

So many people today, including Christian leaders, are caught in noisy lives, hurrying here and there to accomplish what they believe to be the work of God. All the while their souls are increasingly barren for want of true rest. The spiritual guide knows that there is a place of sabbath and restoration for the person making the journey to Christ. It involves a turning away from the trap of performance and silently moving toward the salvation of the Lord which alone brings rest (Isaiah 30:15).

Solitude

John Michael Talbot has written a powerful book about Saint Francis entitled, *The Lessons of Saint Francis: How to Bring Simplicity and Spirituality into Your Daily Life.* In it he writes:

> "By practicing the discipline of solitude, we are creating a space in our lives where God can be with us. And over time, as that space grows, so can our relationship with the living God." [12]

Most people have made very little space for God, filling their lives with people and activities in a desperate effort to keep some distance between themselves and their own brokenness. But the saints of the past, like Francis, believed that solitude was the only way to confront those personal demons.

In solitude a person is able to come to the end of the false self, which enables him to take the first step toward new life and freedom. The spiritual exercise of solitude is much different than isolation. Isolation is about running away to hide and find a semblance of safety. Solitude on the other

[12] Talbot, John Michael and Steve Rabey, *The Lessons of Saint Francis: How to Bring Simplicity and Spirituality into Your Daily Life* (New York, New York: Dutton Books, 1997), p. 63.

hand, is a running toward the truth, confronting it in the power of Christ and returning with joy.

The spiritual guide will find that people do not know what to do in solitude, afraid that it will be boring, a waste of time, or worse, an invitation to personal uneasiness. The spiritual guide should help the person confront such fears, including other spiritual disciplines and exercises in the time of solitude that will open the person's senses to the agenda of God. Sessions following assigned times of solitude are usually ripe for discussion about the challenge that solitude brings to the process of spiritual development.

Symbol

The doctoral course I teach on spiritual guidance usually has about twenty students. The class is made up of men and women who have spent considerable time in ministry and who are now seeking to further equip themselves for service. I love working with these dear people. They are precious children of the Lord, alive in Christ and faithful in service. They arrive straight from the demands of ministry, hungry to grow and learn. Each morning before class I place a symbol at each seat. It might be a cross, religious icon, picture, rock, candle, prayer cloth or other item that has spiritual significance. I then ask them to live with that icon throughout the day, allowing it to draw them to the presence of the Lord.

Not that many years ago I would have run from such an assignment, believing it to be too close to idolatry. But the journey into darkness taught me a great deal about the use of symbols. Again, there is no power in the item itself. It is simply an object that has the potential of pointing an individual to a greater truth. A candle might help a person focus on the fire of the Holy Spirit, or the light of God's presence. A cross could remind an individual of Calvary, or challenge their own willingness to embrace the cost of discipleship. The symbol itself is silent, but the Holy Spirit can use it to speak volumes to the willing heart.

Symbols serve as windows that open by the Spirit to a deeper truth and greater reality. I have symbols throughout my office and often send a person home with one, to contemplate its meaning and be confronted by its message. The spiritual guide should collect many and use them to develop very necessary spiritual sensitivities. Again, every spiritual exercise needs a season of debriefing, a time of dialogue where the person seeking help has opportunity to share if, when, and how they encountered the Lord through the assigned activity.

Sacrament

On the night Jesus was betrayed, He took bread and broke it, saying *"This is my body given for you; do this in remembrance of me"* (Luke 22:19). Later in much the same way He took the cup and said, *"This cup is the new covenant in my blood, which is poured out for you"* (Luke 22:20). Since that Passover night, Christians have gathered to celebrate the Eucharist. Partaking of the Lord's Supper is one of the most important moments in the corporate life of Christians. And as He asked, we do it "in remembrance" of Him.

When I was a pastor, I believed it important that the Eucharist celebration was the most exciting worship service in the congregation's life. I always encouraged people to run, not walk to the table of Christ. On those occasions we saw people saved, healed, reconciled and called into ministry. There is an indescribable power present when people come together to break bread and drink wine in remembrance of the sacrifice of Jesus.

The celebration of the Lord's Supper is important for the spiritual pilgrim. The spiritual guide should encourage understanding and participation in this wonderful act of covenant love. I encourage the spiritual guide to have elements available for use in sessions. In some traditions consecrating the elements can only be done by the ordained clergy. In that case, I encourage the spiritual guide to have pastors pray over the elements before the spiritual guide distributes them.

However accomplished, the spiritual exercise of sacrament is one of the most important ways people are positioned for the transforming touch of Christ.

Spiritual disciplines and spiritual exercises are the tools of spiritual guidance. Chosen through prayer, each has the potential to deeply impact an individual's journey to Christ-likeness. The spiritual guide should seek to incorporate them into his ministry with care and sensitivity. They are in many ways sacred activities that open up space for the presence of God. Treated as such, spiritual disciplines and spiritual exercises soon become precious to the guide and the guided alike.

Chapter 8

Seasons of Change

In 1992 David Hall, Drew Travis and I were on a three-day hunting trip in the Marble Mountains of Northern California. The terrain at seven thousand feet is steep and rugged, but the views are absolutely breathtaking. We especially liked to pack into the basin where Taylor Lake is located. It is isolated, pristine and alive with trout. We set up camp at the edge of the water, enjoying our own private bit of heaven on earth. But without warning, everything changed that day and we were faced with an unexpected storm.

We made our trip into the mountains in early September, when the weather is still warm and the mountains quite inviting. But this afternoon, after we trekked over the high ridge and down into Meeker's Meadow, the weather took a drastic turn. We were caught in a sudden snowstorm that fell hard and fast. There were moments when it was a virtual whiteout and we could not work our way back to camp. I remember huddling under a fir tree, trying to stay as dry as possible. Each of us had dressed that day for warm weather. We wore light clothing, had no gloves and little food, expecting to be back at camp by early afternoon. But we were stuck and we were freezing.

I believe that I was never so cold before or since. My bare hands were turning blue and I was, as they say, chilled to the bone. Drew said that his feet felt like blocks of ice and David was shivering noticeably. The cold set in on that mountain and did not lift. We were miles from camp and the trip out was straight up the side of the mountain. We inched our way along, wondering how we were ever going to make it out. Thankfully, Drew's father, who lived in the town at the base of the mountain, anticipated what had happened and came to greet us on the trail. He brought clothes, food and hot drinks for us all. His attentiveness made up for our mistake. One that we vowed we would never make again.

Seasons Do Change

People must pay attention to changing seasons, for they bring challenges that demand careful preparation and planning. That is not only true with the calendar year; it is also quite true on the journey to Christ-likeness. The movement toward the Lord is a lifelong pilgrimage and the believer will face very different seasons designed by God for specific purposes in his life. Unlike most suffering, which happens because of brokenness and sin, changing seasons are initiated by the Lord. He allows His children to face them as part of their spiritual development and growth. Each holds the potential to strengthen the follower of Christ in very specific ways. But the seeker must know how to respond, or like my friends and me, he might find himself unprepared and in many ways working against what the Lord is doing.

Most Christians will pass through four seasons on the journey to Christ-likeness. As mentioned, these seasons are initiated by the Lord and are designed to perfect believers in Christ. The seasons do not necessarily happen in a certain order. Nor is it possible to anticipate how long one will last. That has more to do with the way each person responds to the season than anything else. Believers will pass through the seasons many times on the life journey, but each time the Lord does a deeper work in every person's life.

It is absolutely essential that the spiritual guide understands the nature and purpose of spiritual seasons. Many Christians do not comprehend what they are all about and as a result react improperly. Well-meaning people will end up giving counsel that does harm to people. The spiritual guide should be the voice of understanding and direction, helping a person position himself for the work that God wants to accomplish through changing times. The changing spiritual seasons are in fact seasons of great change, which I have identified as:

- *the season of delight*
- *the season of distance*
- *the season in the desert*
- *the season of darkness.*

The Season of Delight

In January of 1992, I was reading Psalm 20 and was deeply moved by verse 4. It reads, *"May he give you the desire of your heart."* I felt the Holy Spirit beckoning me to lay before God my deepest desire. For some time He had been igniting within me an ever-increasing passion to know Him more. Worn out by my mismanaging of ministry demands, I wanted to draw closer to God in devotion and love. And so I prayed for a more intimate relationship with Him, marking the date in my Bible as a memorial of remembrance.

Within a few weeks the door opened for me to take a three-month sabbatical from my responsibilities at the church. This afforded me the privilege of spending long periods in prayer and reading Scripture. Day by day the waters of refreshing poured across the parched ground of my soul. Within weeks I could sense an awakening of my spiritual senses. There was a sweetness and delight to those days like I had never known in the past. God was so close in prayer. Scripture came alive as I read, not giving information alone, but drawing me into His presence. This season came as a gift of God's grace, laying a foundation of intimacy upon which my future was to be built. These days initiated a hunger for more of the Lord that helped sustain me through the trials and difficulties yet to come.

The season of delight is reminiscent of the narrative in the Song of Songs. The young girl has been overwhelmed by the presence of her lover. She declared,

> *"I delight to sit in his shade*
> *and his fruit is sweet to my taste.*
> *He has taken me to the banquet hall,*
> *and his banner over me is love.*
> *Strengthen me with raisins,*
> *refresh me with apples,*
> *for I am faint with love.*
> *His left arm is under my head,*
> *and his right arm embraces me."*
>
> (Song of Solomon 2:3–6)

Her words reveal intoxication with the lover's presence and a contentment to rest with him. It is the time of delight, a season of great intimacy and enthusiastic love.

In the mid-seventies there was a small church in rural Pennsylvania where a revival took place among a group of young people. Several dozen teenagers came to confess Christ and were aflame with a genuine passion to know God. For quite some time these youthful zealots were consumed with a most contagious love for the Lord. I remember being moved by their enthusiasm for Bible study, witnessing and most of all prayer meetings. There were times when they spent entire nights in prayer. Throughout this time the sweetness of the Lord's presence was satisfying and so enjoyable to them. It was a season of delight they likely will never forget.

The season of delight is sweet, innocent, exciting and exhilarating. In many ways it could be compared to teenage "puppy love" that seems so complete, so deep, so permanent. Christians would love to stay there forever, content to rest in this level of intimacy with God. It certainly feels new, alive and intoxicating. But God will not allow Christians to remain there. The journey will move on, the seasons will change.

The Father knows that there are far greater experiences of intimacy and harmony awaiting the faithful pilgrim. But reaching those levels of oneness demand more difficult times, when His presence is not as sweet or accessible. There are other seasons along the journey, designed to purge people of anything and everything that does not reflect the nature of Christ. These seasons open a greater space for God deep within, enabling people to contain far more of His priceless treasure. But here, in the season of delight, God allows the intoxicating first taste of His presence that prepares people to seek after Him even more. Make no mistake, this experience of His presence is real, important, and at some levels transforming. But by His grace He will position people for deeper and more consuming encounters of His love.

The spiritual guide must hold a creative tension with people when they move into a season of delight. On one hand there is reason for rejoicing at the wonder and nearness of His love. This must be supported and celebrated. But the spiritual guide is aware that there will be another time, another season along the way, which will not be as easy and exciting. The spiritual guide must prepare for this personally, and position the person seeking help to keep seeking the deeper things of God.

The Season of Distance

Following the beloved's season of delight in her lover's arms comes a period of separation. Without warning, he is gone. Longing for his nearness, she sets out to find him, fired all the more by the memory of his embrace. The beloved goes looking for her betrothed.

> *"All night long on my bed I looked for the one my heart loves;*
>   *I looked for him but did not find him.*
> *I will get up now and go about the city,*
>   *through its streets and squares;*
> *I will search for the one my heart loves.*
>   *So I looked for him but did not find him.*

The watchman found me
as they made their rounds in the city.
'Have you seen the one my heart loves?' "

(Song of Solomon 3:1–3)

There will be times when it seems as though God is far away, unresponsive to prayer, His words of love silent. It may seem as though there is little movement on the journey. Rather than sensing His closeness, the Christian feels that God is not there, not listening, not drawing them into His tender arms. But in this season of distance God is doing a deep work, preparing the seeker for greater transformation. The Lord at times withdraws the sweetness of delight in order to move the believer forward into the depths of forever love.

The Christian mystic Jeanne Guyon has served as spiritual guide to countless people over the centuries. In her classic work, *Experiencing the Depths of Jesus Christ*, she wrote of the season of silence, saying,

> "Now why would God do that? Dear saint of God you must learn the ways of your Lord. Yours is a God who hides Himself. He hides Himself for a purpose. Why? His purpose is to rouse you from spiritual laziness. His purpose in removing Himself from you is to cause you to pursue Him."[13]

The spiritual guide should be aware that many people do not understand what God intends for this season and respond poorly. Anxious by His apparent absence they may become nervous and introspective asking, "What have I done? Where is the sin? What can I do to bring back the delight of His presence? Should I pray more? Repent more? Serve more? What is the key?" These prayers are often driven by a selfish desire to gain control. The season of distance demands, yet

---

[13] Guyon, Jeanne, *Experiencing the Depths of Jesus Christ* (Beaumont, Texas: Seed Sowers Publishers, 1975), p. 27.

again, the stance of surrender and willingness. While prayer, repentance, and service are certainly part of the believer's response to God, they are not the keys to the season of distance. This time of silence does not come because the person has done something wrong. It comes as a work of God designed to bring significant change.

Richard Foster experienced the season of distance in his own spiritual pilgrimage. He wrote about it in *Prayer: Finding the Heart's True Home*:

> "Allow me to share with you one time when I entered the Prayer of the Forsaken. By every outward standard things were going well. Publishers wanted me to write for them. Speaking invitations were too numerous and too gracious. Yet through a series of events it seemed clear to me that God wanted me to retreat from public activity. In essence God was saying, 'Keep quiet!' and so I did. I stopped all public speaking, I stopped all writing, and I waited. At the time this began I did not know if I would ever speak or write again – I rather thought I would not. As it turned out, this fast from public life lasted about eighteen months.
>
> I waited in silence. And God was silent too. I joined in the Psalmist's query: 'How long will you hide your face from me?' (Psalm 13:1). The answer I got: nothing. Absolutely nothing! There were no sudden revelations. No penetrating insights. Not even gentle assurance. Nothing! ... as best as I can discern, the silence of God month after month was a purifying silence."[14]

There is help in understanding the season of distance from Habakkuk. During a time of silence the prophet continued to cry out before the Lord, while staying faithful to stand his post as a watchman of Israel. God's apparent distance did not lead

---

[14] Foster, Richard, *Prayer: Finding the Hearts True Home* (San Francisco, California: HarperSanFrancisco, 1992), pp. 20, 21.

Habakkuk to run in panic, but instead he waited in faithful anticipation (Habakkuk 2:1). That is always the response of faith. Those seeking God must be encouraged to continue the journey in faith, coming to Him in worship and devotion, trusting that in His appointed time God's nearness will again be experienced. The spiritual guide should encourage the person they are helping to speak every concern and desire to the Father and then wait. He is doing a work far beyond sense and comprehension. In the season of distance, the Lord is still very active, shaping the believer into the image of His Son, Jesus Christ.

The Season in the Desert

All Christians go through desert experiences along the journey toward Christ-likeness. They are seasons of testing and character building that are foundational to spiritual growth. Nothing will help the spiritual guide, or those they help, understand such times better than the biblical narrative of Israel's journey from Egypt to Canaan. Following four hundred years of bondage, God set His people free to journey to a new home. Under Moses' leadership, God set them on a course to the Promised Land, but they were to pass through a savage wilderness. There, apart from the normal provisions of life, God was determined to shape His people so that they would live in Canaan as His holy and obedient nation.

The season in the desert brought hunger, thirst, enemy threat and devastating boredom. It was also a time when God would call them to trust His love and have faith in His provision for their lives. But they were a rebellious people. As a result, incessant doubt, division and constant complaining extended their stay in the desert for forty years. Many who began the journey to the Promised Land never arrived. They died in the dust of an endless wilderness.

Seasons in the desert are quite similar for Christians today. They are times of character building, during which the many comforts of faith Christians normally take for granted are noticeably absent. The purpose of the season of desert is clear. It is a time and place of stripping away. All the things believers normally count on for safety and security are out of reach. The things they do to kill the pain of rejection, or abuse, or loneliness do not seem to work any more. Like Israelites without leeks and onions, people begin to want the false gods they have created in order to feel good again.

This was most certainly true when it came to the core abandonment and loneliness I felt deep inside. Very early on I had touched that deep pain and it was devastating, so much so that I never wanted to feel that way again. And if I even got close to that horrible feeling I would grab for the pain-killers and take all I could to numb those dark, devastating emotions. I could stay away from the pain of abandonment and loneliness through performance, building co-dependent relationships with certain people and distancing from others. I could also distract myself from the pain through a variety of activities, like sports, reading, work, movies, a good meal, or sex. Whenever the circumstance of my life situation brought me close to that deep dark place, I would escape through one of my painkillers.

In his book, *Reaching Out*, Henri Nouwen wrote about this tendency to mask the pain of our own loneliness:

> "Too often we will do everything possible to avoid the confrontation with the experience of being alone, and sometimes are able to create the most ingenious devices to prevent ourselves from being reminded of this con-dition. Our culture has become most sophisticated in the avoidance of pain, not only our physical pain, but our emotional pain as well. We not only bury our dead as though they are still alive, but we also bury our pains as if they were not really there. We have become so used to this state of anesthesia, that we panic when there is nothing or nobody left to distract us. When we have no project to finish, no friend to visit, no book to read, no television to watch or no record to play, and when we are left all

alone by ourselves we are brought so close to the revelation of our basic human aloneness and are so afraid of experiencing an all pervasive sense of loneliness that we will do anything to get busy again and continue the game which makes us believe that everything is fine after all."[15]

False gods must be cast down and destroyed so that trust in the living God can increase. The Father is truly near in the season of desert, beckoning people to receive His love and provisions for life. He asks believers to open their clenched fist holding their own household gods and move toward His embrace. The season of desert can become a time of His miraculous intervention into daily life, if the Christian is able to exercise trust and obedience.

The spiritual guide can be a great help to people who are in the season of desert. He can help position people to move on toward the land of God's promise and abundance. Psalm 106 offers great advice on how to respond to the season of desert and should be used by the spiritual guide when offering help. There are, within the psalm, thirteen principles that position people for God's provision in the season of desert:

- Believe His promises (v. 12)
- Sing His praise (v. 12)
- Remember what He has done for you in the past (v. 13)
- Seek His counsel (v. 13)
- Do not give in to sinful desires (v. 14)
- Do not envy others (v. 16)
- Do not turn to familiar idols (v. 19)
- Do not despise the place God has put you in (v. 24)
- Do not grumble (v. 25)
- Obey the Lord (v. 25)
- Do not strike out in anger (v. 33)
- Cry out to God in humility (v. 44)
- Praise the Lord! (v. 48)

[15] Nouwen, Henri, *Reaching Out*, p. 27.

The spiritual guide can use this text to help people respond to the season of desert in ways that position them for the transforming touch of the Father.

The Season of Darkness

No season is as difficult to bear as the season of darkness. Saint John of the Cross called such times, "The dark night of the soul." And rightly so. The dark night of the soul can be painful and debilitating. There will be moments of great doubt, fear and challenges that threaten to undo a person's faith. Larry Crabb has written that, "Disappointment, severe enough to be called death is unavoidable in a true spiritual journey."[16] I am not completely sure that all Christians pass through this time. But many have, and those that do know that it is real, dark and very difficult. The season of darkness is a time of brokenness that eventually leads to incredible change and blessings. It is the Christian equivalent of chrysalis, a time of deep transformation in a place of personal darkness.

During the time of difficulty and oppression, God is at work, revealing impure motives and character sins that greatly affect a person's relationship with Him. God will possibly point out such sins as pride, anger and a preoccupation with importance. He will also expose weak places in the foundation of a person's faith that desperately needed addressing. This season of weakness and suffering often shapes an entirely new approach to the journey of life.

The psalmist blessed the Lord for the time of affliction, saying that it put him back on course with God (Psalm 119:67, 75). Paul declared that a dark time in his own life birthed a greater dependence on the Lord (2 Corinthians 1:9). He taught the early Christians that suffering produced the necessary qualities of Christ in their lives (Romans 5:1–5). And James, the brother of our Lord went so far as to tell people to

---

[16] Crabb, Larry, *The Safest Place on Earth* (Nashville, Tennessee: Word Publishing, 1999), p. 5.

rejoice in trial, because the outcomes were priceless to their strength (James 1:2–4). These are but a few of the countless texts which teach that God at times allows pain and suffering as a means of transforming a person's life.

Saint John of the Cross, in *Dark Night of the Soul*, concluded that there were several reasons why God allows such suffering in a believer's life, including to:

* Forge humility
* Put people in touch with their inherent weakness
* Exalt God's greatness
* Break pride
* Purify the soul
* Set people free from spiritual laziness
* Teach deeper spiritual truths
* Help people pursue God rather than the things of God.

Saint John of the Cross believed that the season of darkness forged a level of intimacy like nothing else possibly could do. He also knew that the difficulties of that season would transform the surrendered believer into the likeness of Christ.[17] These are both aspects of spiritual development that the seeker must say "yes" to, even in the time of great difficulty.

The spiritual guide must be available and attentive when someone is going through the season of darkness. It is a frightening time and more than a few Christians have made very poor decisions during that season. Listening, supporting, encouraging and loving the seeker are all of paramount importance. The season of darkness is also a time when the person needs to be encouraged to express hurts, fears and frustrations to the Lord. The psalmists did this regularly, which invited the presence of God into the time of great pain. The spiritual guide would do well to assign psalms of lament to the person during times of trial and disappointment. They

---

[17] These principles were gleaned from *The Dark Night of the Soul*, by St. John of the Cross, published in New York by Doubleday, in 1990.

will serve to direct the individual's own lament up to the Lord.

Once again, pat answers do no one any good during the season of darkness. The spiritual guide must allow the Holy Spirit to lead every step of the way. The person in the dark night may want to act out. The spiritual guide should be patient and prayerful, providing a safe, accepting environment during this journey through the dark. The season will end and the Lord will reveal His presence once again. The journey of life will continue and the spiritual guide will have new opportunities to serve the seeker in the ongoing pursuit of Christ and His likeness.

I am well aware that identifying the four seasons is simply a way of helping people understand the different ways the Lord shapes a person on the journey of life. They serve as a metaphorical description of the observable activity of the Lord along the path to Christ and His likeness. The Father has willed that all believers move toward that great destination. Times of delight, distance, desert and darkness do happen and they serve the "all things" plan of God. The spiritual guide will need to help people understand this activity of the Father. Surrender and willingness will be essential. But in the end, the time of pain will become a source of great blessing. Individuals will, with ever increasing glory, be transformed into the likeness of Jesus. Can there be a greater privilege than to help people move toward such wonderful change? Is there any greater responsibility?

Chapter 9

Enemies in the Darkness

Christians today are quite anxious to embrace a balanced understanding and approach to the topic of spiritual warfare. They have heard enough from the two extremes, those who either see a demon behind every bush, or believe it is all myth and madness. They want to be able to treat the topic with integrity and develop strategies that actually work against the powers of evil. They are tired of being blindsided by the evil one and are anxious to learn about the power of Christ that sets the captive free. It is with those people in mind that I write this chapter. I intend that the treatment be biblical, understandable and practical. And the focus will be directed to the work of spiritual guidance and the presence of enemies that lay wait in the dark places along the journey of life.

There will likely be some readers who may be uncomfortable about including a discussion on spiritual warfare in a book on spiritual guidance. After all, it is seldom integrated into material on that subject. I have well over one hundred books on my shelf that are either about spiritual guidance as a calling, or directed at providing spiritual guidance to others. Less than ten percent of those even remotely address the issue. Only two include a serious treatment of the topic. Why? I must admit that I am not completely sure. It may be that the modern view of reality has shaped the authors' attitudes about there being an actual spirit realm. Others might avoid the subject because it does open the door to some level of controversy. There may even be those who feel it is simply not directly relevant to the discipline of spiritual formation. Regardless, I would feel irresponsible to not integrate such a critical discussion into a volume aimed at equipping people to help others make the journey toward Christ. And the best starting point is with the attitude of Jesus toward this topic.

Jesus and Spiritual Warfare

There are repeated references to the devil, evil spirits and the ministry of deliverance in the gospel accounts of the Lord's ministry.[18] It is unquestionable that Jesus took seriously the presence of evil spirits in the world, since He dedicated a significant amount of His time to setting people free from their destructive influences. His confrontation with the forces of darkness began after Jesus was baptized by John the Baptist. He went in to the desert for forty days of fasting and prayer and there was tempted by Satan. The evil one was intent upon luring Jesus away from the path God had set before Him. Satan tried three times to influence Christ to choose another way. But the Lord was unwilling to step aside one inch from the journey ahead. He rebuked the devil with the Word of God and stayed the course. The forces of darkness will seek to use that same strategy against believers as they journey toward Christ-likeness. The spiritual guide must be able to help them resist as Jesus did.

Jesus certainly did not question the existence of evil spirits. There are numerous stories in the gospel accounts about Christ confronting demonic activity as part of His healing ministry (Mark 1:32–24; Matthew 8:16; Luke 4:40–41). There are also specific stories about people being delivered from evil spirits, including the Gadarene demoniac (Mark 5:2–20), Mary Magdalene (Mark 16:19), the man who could not speak

---

[18] Certain sections of the material included in this chapter can also be found in my book *Healing Care, Healing Prayer*, published by Leafwood Publishers in 2001. The discussion in that volume, however, is focused upon evil supernaturalism as it relates to the ministry of inner healing prayer. Here I have redirected the material to fit the topic of spiritual guidance.

(Matthew 9:32–34), and the boy who experienced repeated seizures (Matthew 17:14–22).

When Jesus called His disciples, He gave them authority to cast out demons (Matthew 10:1). The book of Acts gives ample evidence that they did in fact include deliverance as part of their ministry (Acts 5:16; 8:7; 16:16–18). One particularly interesting story is found in Acts 19:13–16. It seems that the seven sons of a man named Sceva tried to invoke the name of Jesus in an effort to deliver a man who was demon possessed. Interestingly, the demon spirit spoke saying, *"Jesus I know, and I know about Paul, but who are you?"* (v. 15). With that, the man with the evil spirit jumped on them and beat them until they ran away bruised and naked. This story certainly encourages Christians to understand the nature of spiritual warfare and how to deal with evil spirits when they attack people on the journey through life.

The New Testament teaches that evil spirits exist and that they,

> Are evil (Luke 11:24–26)
> Intend to do harm (Mark 9:17–18)
> Accuse (Revelation 12:10–11)
> Deceive (1 Timothy 4:1)
> Bring sickness and disease (Mark 5:2–4)
> Torment people (Mark 5:1–18)

While this reality may initially frighten believers, they should never run in fear or pretend that evil spirits do not exist. The spiritual guide must especially understand the nature of their schemes and help people stand boldly in the power of Christ. In his book, *Demon Possession and the Christian*, Fred Dickason assures Christians that demon powers are limited by God and ultimately overcome by the blood of Christ.

> "Despite the awesome powers of Satan and demons, believers may confidently rest in their sovereign Creator and Savior. He defeated Satan's hosts at the cross, controls

all things, and guarantees in His wisdom, love, and faithfulness that He will never leave us or forsake us. Neither can any demon separate us from the love of Christ (Colossians 2:15; Hebrews 13:5). The demons believe and tremble (James 2:19). Believers may believe and trust."[19]

These words are a comfort to the soul, and should encourage the spiritual guide to learn more about this issue and the authority that is available through Jesus Christ.

The Apostle Paul warned the believers of Ephesus that many of the struggles they encountered in life were ultimately rooted in spiritual forces (Ephesians 6:12). Practically, this means that there are times when people on the journey toward Christ are being bothered by dark forces determined to stop their progress. They will try to influence people to go another way, tempt them to say "yes" to sinful responses to life and throw up obstacles to growing in the Lord. These spiritual forces are evil, care nothing about what is good and right, and will use anyone or anything to damage those who love the Lord. The spiritual guide must take this matter seriously, for lives are harmed when evil is given free reign.

The question is of course, how do evil spirits attack believers as they journey toward Christ-likeness? In general, they seek to distract and dissuade people from following the Lord. They do this in a wide variety of ways, which I categorize as follows:

- *Harassment*: Much the same as a hornet flies around a person's head, annoying and distracting a person, the evil spirit does not keep the person away from his or her appointed course, but does seek to bother and discourage them.
- *Oppression*: This type of attack from an evil spirit is much like a fog that settles in upon a person. The individual

[19] Dickason, C. Fred, *Demon Possession and the Christian* (Westchester, Illinois: Crossway, 1987), pp. 30–31.

finds it more difficult to stay on track and often battles varying levels of emotional and spiritual oppression. It can be more difficult for a person to keep focused on the presence and power of Christ.

- *Affliction*: Jesus often cast out demons when people suffered from physical sickness. At this level of activity, evil spirits seek to bring emotional, spiritual and physical suffering to a person in an effort to defeat and demoralize them on the journey toward Christ.

- *Bondage*: In this level of attack the evil spirit is exercising a certain level of control in an area of a person's life. This is only possible when personal choices give room for this type of bondage. This level of problem demands significant help, even to the point of deliverance.

The spiritual guide should be aware that there can and often are other reasons for individuals to struggle in life. The normal obstacles of living in a fallen world are themselves tough to handle. Most of the time people end up is trouble simply because of the poor choices they make, but there are also enemies in the darkness, seeking to influence and manipulate matters toward the destruction of people's lives. The spiritual guide needs to seek the Holy Spirit's help in discerning the degree to which an individual is the object of an evil scheme from forces in the spiritual realm. The strategy for dealing with this type of problem must be rooted in the power of Jesus Christ and His victory on Calvary.

Equipping People to Stand Against the Enemies in the Darkness

The effective spiritual guide will seek to help people understand and combat the strategies of evil forces that align against them. Regardless of the level of attack, be it harassment, oppression, affliction, or bondage, the person moving toward Christ-likeness should be equipped to resist and stay on course with Christ. I would recommend that the spiritual guide both knows and teaches these six truths that relate to spiritual warfare:

- *the victory of Christ*
- *stay empowered*
- *be well armed and dangerous*
- *stay alert*
- *stay prayerful*
- *never give ground for evil.*

Each will be discussed in the remainder of this chapter.

The victory of Christ

The Bible teaches emphatically that the evil one is a defeated foe. Jesus Christ has won the victory over all the powers of darkness and He did it for every person who is on the journey toward His likeness. While the battle is real, the victory is complete and secure. Believers do not need to be helpless victims of the devil. Jesus has made every necessary provision for the daily journey, including the power and means to resist evil. The spiritual guide must equip the person seeking help to understand spiritual warfare. People can be taught to carefully and fearlessly walk in the light of God's Word. Instructing people to meditate on the following promises and instructions that come from Scripture is an excellent place to start.

> "... God made you alive with Christ. He forgave us all our sins, having canceled the written code, with its regulations, that was against us and that stood opposed to us; he took it away nailing it to the cross. And having disarmed the powers and authorities, he made a public spectacle of them, triumphing over them by the cross."   (Colossians 2:13–15)

> "... he too shared in their humanity, so that by his death he might destroy him who holds the power of death – that is, the devil."   (Hebrews 2:14)

"You, dear children, are from God and have overcome [evil spirits], *because the one who is in you is greater than the one who is in the world."* (1 John 4:4)

"... the Lord is faithful, and he will strengthen and protect you from the evil one." (2 Thessalonians 3:3)

"The Lord will rescue me [Paul] *from every evil attack and will bring me safely to his heavenly kingdom. To him be glory for ever and ever. Amen."* (2 Timothy 4:18)

The testimony of Scripture is full of such passages, assuring believers that His strong arm is mighty to save. The spiritual guide and those they help need to be serious about the battle, but never fearful. The Lord Jesus Christ has made a way for victory, promising that in the end God will crush the evil one under your feet (Romans 16:20).

Stay empowered

The Apostle Paul admonished followers of Christ to *"be strong in the Lord and in his mighty power"* (Ephesians 6:10). He was not at all suggesting this as a theological topic to be debated and discussed in the classroom. Paul knew that strong forces were aligned against the followers of Christ, bent on defeating and destroying them all. Satan is not a little horned character that sits on one's shoulder whispering naughty suggestions. He is the prince of darkness and works savagely to stop people on the journey to Christ. He is full of vile hatred toward God and despises every person who has confessed faith. The evil one is real, dangerous and the leader of minions of fallen angels headed for eternal night. But before that day, each spirit is dedicated to stopping any movement toward Christ-likeness.

The spiritual guide should continually emphasize to those they help that walking in victory takes supernatural power. The seeker should regularly position himself for the ongoing infilling of the Holy Spirit who brings that power to life. The battle of flesh and blood is not a war of words and ideas. It is a struggle against dark forces in high places and as such the combatant needs to be supported by the power of God. Those followers who have been touched by the schemes of evil know that they need to stay strong in the Lord. They realize that they must walk in the strength of His might. Anything less is an invitation to disaster. The spiritual guide must point to the reality of this cosmic battle and encourage Christians to ask for that power and never stop asking.

Be well armed and dangerous

One of the most important teachings about spiritual warfare in Scripture comes from Paul's letter to the Ephesians, chapter 6, verses 10–19. Throughout the history of the church, Christians have turned there for help against the attacks of Satan. This passage is central to any discussion of the conflict between evil and the Christian. It offers key and practical insight and advice on how to stand strong during difficult times. It is obvious from reading the text that Paul wanted believers to be well equipped to stand against the schemes of the evil one. He saw no reason for Christians to stand naked and defenseless against the onslaught of Satan's attack. Personally, I go over the essentials of Paul's instructions most days during prayer. I would not even consider moving out in life and ministry without arming myself as he suggests.

With reference to spiritual warfare, Paul admonishes believers to put on the full armor of God in order to fight the evil one. He then lists very specific pieces of armor, using them as metaphorical images of arming oneself for battle. Paul uses imagery from warfare because he knows that the enemy is real and violent against God's children. He wants believers to be prepared for battle at all times. Each piece of armor represents a central truth that the believer must embrace daily, to press back the enemies that hide in the darkness. He lists them as:

- *The belt of truth* (v. 14)
- *The breastplate of righteousness* (v. 14)

- *The shoes of peace* (v. 15)
- *The shield of faith* (v. 16)
- *The helmet of salvation* (v. 17)
- *The sword of the Spirit* (v. 17)

The spiritual guide should not only stay armed himself, but instruct all he helps to do the same. To daily pray on the armor of the Lord is an exercise of confession and declaration, letting all spiritual forces, good and evil, know that a person is moving forward on the journey to Christ, with Christ!

Stay alert

Making a journey through hostile territory demands that a person remain watchful at all times. Christians would do well to remember that this world is under enemy occupation and that every step on the journey of life is made in full view of evil forces. While some may feel that is an over-dramatization, it is far from it. The amount of suffering caused by evil in this world is staggering. At every single level of human existence there is the potential for great hurt. The evil one does lie in wait and so the person moving forward in Christ must learn how to recognize his schemes. Paul urged believers to stay alert against the forces of darkness (Ephesians 6:18).

I know that believers can seek the help of the Holy Spirit in discerning the presence of evil. I have experienced that myself, sensing a deep internal warning that something is amiss and I need to be especially on my guard. Scripture does use a variety of metaphors to identify the ways of evil that can provide significant help in learning to spot the enemy:

- **The ruler of this world** (1 John 5:18–19): Satan often works through the governmental and societal structures of this world to do violence to the Kingdom of God. Political oppression and persecution of every type bring great harm to countless lives.
- **The prince of the power of the air** (Ephesians 2:2 KJV): There is a spiritual hierarchy of demon powers that seek

to harass, deceive, destroy and deceive people. Though unseen, they are ever active and under the ultimate authority of Satan himself.

- *An angel of light* (2 Corinthians 11:14): The evil one often appears in very good, religious ways, even presenting a very moral presence. The truth is, he is using the appearance of light to draw people into ultimate darkness. While cults are an obvious example of this, various extremes of legalism, intellectualism, liberalism and religious emotionalism can also be affected by his schemes.
- *A roaring lion* (1 Peter 5:8): Satan hurls threats of destruction and harm, hoping to get people to isolate from God's flock so he can devour them. It is critical that Christians maintain unity against evil, shoulder to shoulder and close to God.
- *Slanderer* (1 Timothy 5:14): Evil spirits love to capitalize on people's proclivity for gossip by igniting controversy through slander, rumor and suspicion. Many fine Christians have been damaged because weaker believers fell pray to this all too familiar tactic.
- *Accuser* (Revelation 12:10): Jesus Christ has forgiven believers of every wrong, every sin and every failure. Yet Satan will constantly try to make people feel condemned, worthless and guilty before God. These feelings in the Christian's life never originate with God. The enemy knows that getting people to doubt God's unconditional love leads to very self-destructive behavior.

The spiritual guide must help people keep watch against the work of evil. The journey to Christ-likeness will be opposed, but united in the power of Jesus, believers can move on to personal victory.

Stay prayerful

In Paul's discussion of spiritual warfare he urged believers to pray every chance they had and to use every form of prayer possible (Ephesians 6:18). Prayer matters! I admittedly do not understand everything about the relationship of spiritual power and prayer, but I know it is there and it is important. Somehow prayer pushes a hole through heaven and allows the cries of God's children to be clearly heard. When those prayers are received at the throne, the Father responds with angelic forces dispatched to serve the ones He loves. The spiritual guide must make all types of prayer part of the journey.

Paul's specific admonition in Ephesians is that believers *"Pray in the Spirit . . . with all kinds of prayers"* (Ephesians 6:18). Praying in the Spirit means that certain prayers are initiated by the Holy Spirit who is alive within the believer. They pour forth from His presence, shaped by His wisdom and understanding, wed to the needs of the praying person. The Holy Spirit empowers these pleas before God, giving them the necessary force to accomplish the work of the Kingdom. Praying in the Spirit takes on a dimension that is noticeably different from normal prayer. There is unusual power and effectiveness against the strategies of the evil one when the Holy Spirit infills the seeker's prayers.

Paul not only said to pray in the Spirit, but he also told people to pray all kinds of prayer when engaged in spiritual warfare. What does he mean by that? I think he is suggesting that standing against evil involves engaging prayer in several different ways.[20] For example:

- *United prayer*: While each believer has power against the evil one, there is a dynamic increase of strength when Christians unite in prayer. Somehow it dramatically increases the combat power aimed against the enemy in the moment. In the Old Testament when God's people united together they could rout an army. Moses said that two Israelites joined in battle could chase ten thousand (Deuteronomy 32:30). United prayer joins faith to faith,

[20] This material on prayer is taken in part from my book, *Draw Close to the Fire: Finding God in Darkness*, published by Leafwood Publishers.

bringing increased courage in the time of battle. In difficult times believers must call brothers and sisters to get on their knees and fight!

- *Agreeing prayer*: Jesus told His disciples that *"if two of you on earth agree about anything you ask for, it will be done for you by my Father in heaven"* (Matthew 18:19). Jesus said that Christians in agreement have the power to bind and loose things on both heaven and earth. Agreement can invite the presence of Christ into the context of prayer, taking the potential of prayer to an entirely new level. Agreement prayer brings harmony, unity and shared union among the people involved. Agreement provides a united and irresistible front against the forces of darkness.

- *Persevering prayer*: In warfare prayer, people learn to never give up until the breakthrough comes. Jesus told a parable once about a man who needed bread from his friend. He went to him late at night to make his request and the friend said that it was an inconvenient time to meet his need. But the man persevered until finally his friend gave him the bread (Luke 11:5–8). Jesus told His followers to be like that in prayer. Sometimes the oppressive power of evil is not instantly pressed back. In warfare prayer, Christians persistently continue making their request known, trusting the Lord's ultimate victory.

- *Intercessory prayer*: Warfare prayer is not relegated to personal issues exclusively. There are times when the Lord burdens believers with the issues others are facing. Seeing that they are overwhelmed or at risk, He will call people to intercede for them in prayer. This is a ministry of great privilege, for it models the very ministry of Jesus on Christians' behalf. The Bible says that He intercedes for us before the throne of God (Hebrews 7:25). Believers in turn are called to stand in the gap for brothers and sisters in much the same way.

- *The prayer of praise*: Praise is a powerful weapon against the enemy. In the face of the evil one's violent schemes, Christians must unite with songs and declarations of honor, glory and adoration. Believers can gather to praise as a way of combating illness, divorce, job loss, rebellion, poverty and racism. Praise releases the brilliant glory of God and the darkness must flee, or be absolutely destroyed.

The spiritual guide has an opportunity to teach those seeking help about the marvelous power of prayer. May all believers be equipped to, *". . . pray in the Spirit on all occasions with all kinds of prayers and requests"* (Ephesians 6:18).

Never give ground for evil!

Charles Kraft has influenced my thinking about the nature of demonic activity. He always says that demons are like rats. They are attracted to garbage. If you kick out the rats but leave the garbage, they will come back. Jesus said that when they do return, uglier and meaner rats (demons) will join them (Luke 11:24–26). Things only get worse. The importance of this point should never be underestimated. Choosing to do that which is contrary to the Father's will gives ground for the evil one to stand in a person's life. It makes rooms for rats and no believer should ever want that.

People need to be encouraged by the spiritual guide to deal with the sin in their lives. I am convinced that a great deal of the trouble that occurs along the way happens because Christians fall short of the Lord's commands. They make room for demons to do their evil work. That ground must be taken back and surrendered to the Lordship of Jesus Christ. The garbage, to once again use that metaphor, must be cleared and the evil one chased away by the power of Christ. This clearing of ground happens through acts of repentance, renunciation and realignment. Repentance means that a person turns away from the sin that has entrapped them. The Holy Spirit willingly reveals such acts and attitudes and will empower people to turn toward Christ.

Renunciation is an act of declaration essential to cleansing ground. It has been practiced for centuries in the Orthodox

Church, most often at the time of baptism. Renunciation involves a clear statement, taking all ground from the evil one caused by one's sinful actions and proclaiming obedience to Christ. It is a powerful act that leads to tremendous freedom. The final movement involves realigning one's life according to the will of God. Individuals must turn away from sin and toward obedience. Many times this involves ceasing certain behaviors and attitudes that do not reflect the Lord and embracing those that do.

Spiritual warfare is inevitable on the journey toward Jesus Christ. As long as Christians live on this side of the Kingdom, they will encounter enemies in the darkness. It is so important that the spiritual guide has a healthy, balanced understanding of this issue. Countless believers are being deeply harmed by unseen forces bent on their ultimate destruction. The spiritual guide must teach people to be filled with the power of Christ, standing in His victory against evil. Helping people get armed, stay alert, and pray, will serve them long after the relationship with a spiritual director ends. That type of lasting help is what this ministry is all about. People will be free to move toward Christ-likeness in the glorious strength of the Father's great love.

Conclusion

The Joy of the Journey

I love *Christian History* magazine and anxiously await every edition. Four times each year a new volume is published, focusing upon some important period, person, or movement in the history of Christianity. The articles are well written, carefully researched and quite balanced, including pictures and illustrations that bring the stories to life. My favorite section within the magazine is called *The Gallery*. Whenever a volume is dedicated to a particular person, like Martin Luther, Jonathan Edwards, William Wilberforce, or John Wesley, the editors include several pages about contemporaries who played important roles in these people's lives. While most of the individuals discussed in *The Gallery* are unknown today, they were vitally important to the giants of the faith being discussed in the magazine.

Take, for example, the 1990 edition of *Christian History* that focused upon the life and ministry of D.L. Moody. Countless people around the world have heard about this nineteenth-century evangelist who is said to have reached millions with the gospel. But few people would recognize the names of "Auntie" Sarah Cooke and John V. Farwell, yet without them there may have never been the Dwight Lyman Moody history has come to know. According to *The Gallery*, "Auntie" Sarah Cooke, herself a fervent evangelist, was burdened to pray for Moody to receive the baptism of the Holy Spirit. "Auntie" Sarah told D.L. Moody that she and her friend Mrs Hawxhurst were seeking the Lord on his behalf. Moody asked to join them in prayer and eventually had an encounter with the Holy Spirit while in New York City that forever changed his life. Moody later said that his great effectiveness as a preacher was directly linked to that experience.

John V. Farwell was a successful businessman who met D.L. Moody when he was beginning his Sunday School ministry in Chicago. Impressed by the young Moody's earnestness, Farwell signed on to support his efforts. This led to a lifelong association between the two men. Farwell actually designed and built the Chicago Tabernacle as a place where Moody could hold revivals. Farwell supported D.L. Moody to such a degree that many felt he was responsible for much of his success. But John V. Farwell always gave that glory to God alone. But undoubtedly God used Farwell, "Auntie" Sarah Cooke, and many other people in Moody's life. His may be the name most notable to Christians today, but these unsung heroes of the faith played an integral part in his ministry.

Reading about people in *The Gallery* challenges me in two distinct, yet interrelated ways. First, I am reminded that there are many people who support me in ministry. Whatever success and effectiveness I may have is a direct consequence of many unnamed men and women who are constant in prayer, faithful with encouragement and generous with time and personal resources. That has been true for my entire Christian life. Even as I write this chapter I am aware of my wife's love and support, Anne's gifted intercession, Lynne's tireless help and John's daily encouragement. The names and faces of people down through thirty years of ministry flood my mind. I have never been alone on this journey. Many people have walked with me every step of the way.

There are several ways in which my name is the only one people connect with a particular aspect of my ministry. When I speak at a conference, it is my name on the brochure. The books I publish have my name on the covers. Outside my office is a brass plate that again has only my name upon it. But none of that gives a true picture of my life and ministry. There is a gallery of people who have made that possible, and not to any small degree. I have grown to love these saints dearly and am flooded with gratitude and humility when I reflect upon all they have given, with joy. I am certainly a most blessed man because of them.

I am also challenged to consider another truth. I have had countless opportunities to be an unknown face in the galleries of other people. Have I honored that privilege? Did I faithfully serve those who turned my way? Prayerfully? Joyfully? If they were making a list of people who cared and supported their lives, would I be included? Faces begin to appear in my mind, precious men and women who asked for help along the journey of life. There are far too many to even begin naming, yet each person was a child of the King, turning to me for spiritual guidance. Few, if any, knew that I served these people, since the context was private and out of public view. They came to me often in secret, asking for help in times of great challenge and trial.

Many of those who came were pastors, teachers, counselors and laypeople who themselves serve thousands of people. Those being touched by their ministries do not know my name. Most have no idea that I even played a part in their lives. I am simply in the gallery, one of many who helped them along the way. Yet, in countless ways, the time I spent with them in hidden moments was the most important of my life. They were also the most fruitful, unquestionably. Others may point to my public ministries and give honor or recognition. But I know that the help I was able to provide in the quiet moments is far more likely to last into eternity than what I have done in the public eye. That is the nature of God's Kingdom, and always will be. Like Paul, I remember these special people with great thanks and whenever I pray for them I am overcome with joy (Philippians 1:3–4).

Full of Joy

The man or woman who becomes a spiritual guide is invited to a journey of joy. There may not be public recognition and there will certainly be few accolades. But there will be times of great rejoicing. Spiritual guides have the privilege of helping people move closer to Christ and with every step forward there comes a level of gratitude and satisfaction that is at the same time humbling and exhilarating. There will certainly be challenges and trials along the way. But it is not the pain that the spiritual guide remembers, it is the wonderful memory of watching people change, becoming more and more like Jesus on the journey of life.

Three years ago I began a journey with Amy, the daughter of an old friend. She was working in a New York City law firm and had strayed far from the Lord. This deeply concerned her parents. Amy had not been attending church for some time and was making lifestyle choices that were bringing pain to her life. She felt alone, angry and in many ways trapped. Desperate for change, and at her father's recommendation, Amy asked me for help. Today, Amy is married, the mother of little Kyle, living in a small southern town and alive in Christ. She decided to stop working for money and is now serving the hurting and poor with her gifts. I had a front row seat to her personal transformation, watching as the Holy Spirit made all things new in Amy's life. To even think of her brings me an indescribable joy, the overflow of how the Lord feels about her dear life. That is the privilege of being a spiritual guide: joy unspeakable.

Jesus knew this joy. It is written about in the gospel of Luke. The Lord had commissioned seventy-two followers to go into the surrounding towns and villages, telling them that the harvest was plentiful, but the laborers were few (Luke 10:1–24). After giving them detailed instructions, Jesus sent them out two by two. When they returned from their journey, the seventy-two were filled with joy. They had done as Jesus instructed and were excited by the results. They told Jesus all about their experiences and said with amazement, *"... even the demons submit to us in your name"* (Luke 10:17).

The Bible says that Jesus was overcome by joy in the Holy Spirit and spontaneously began to praise the Father in heaven

(Luke 10:21–23). He knew that His followers had made a step forward in Kingdom ministry and He was genuinely thrilled for them. I can imagine Jesus laughing as they each told stories of what happened in the towns and villages. His heart was filled with gratitude and as a result He had to thank God for what they experienced. Jesus had looked forward to this day, when the poor and the outcast turned to bring life and light to the lost and broken. It was a moment of victory as Jesus saw evil defeated and the Kingdom advance through the lives of those He loved and served (Luke 10:18–19). This story is what spiritual guidance is all about.

In an earlier discussion it was suggested that serving as a spiritual guide is in some ways like being a parent. It involves a great deal of nurture, encouragement and instruction, much the same as a father and mother do for a child. And, staying with that metaphor, there are serious challenges along the way and inevitable frustrations. But there are also moments when incredible joy washes through, leaving the deepest feelings of pride and thankfulness. As a parent, I know what I am talking about.

Two years ago, our son Aaron and his wife Destry walked across the platform at graduation and received Master of Divinity degrees. The president allowed me to hand them their diplomas in the ceremony. I was so overcome with emotion that I could barely stand. When I looked into their eyes I felt a love that was deeper than the deepest sea. It was one of the most joyful moments of my life. Granted, there had been more than a few struggles and frustrations along the way. There were times when, as a parent, I had trouble keeping my mouth shut about some matters that I thought needed addressing. I can attribute more than a few gray hairs to Aaron particularly. But on that day, that passed away, and all that remained was tremendous joy. I will soon be privileged to have that same experience with my daughter Cara and her husband Brad. And later I will tear up yet again as our daughter Emily makes her graduation walk. That is the reward of a parent and I intend to receive it in full.

Being a spiritual guide is much like that. After tremendous struggles, attacks from the evil one, challenges that threaten to undo all that one has done to help, a person moves forward toward Christ. The spiritual guide is overcome with joy as he watches a person first sense the presence of the Holy Spirit for themselves. Or he is there when, after hours of teaching, the individual exercises discernment and avoids a trap of the evil one. And few things touch the heart as when a spiritual guide listens as a person describes hearing the whispers of God in their own soul and willingly surrendering to His command. Nothing will compare to those special moments when a spiritual guide realizes that the person he has helped offers God even the darkest moments as opportunities for the Holy Spirit's transforming grace.

The spiritual guide is invited to be full of joy in the Holy Spirit, just as the Lord was on that day so long ago. And in that moment, possibly more than ever before, it will be not about the spiritual guide. The focus will not be upon the spiritual guide's gifting, or expertise, or importance along the way. It will be all about the person being helped. They will be the center of attention, theirs the name that is celebrated, they the individuals getting the reward. The spiritual guide will simply be in the gallery, watching with a depth of joy and gratitude that few things in life afford. The sense of fulfillment will be overwhelming. It is a rare and wonderful privilege to help another person along the journey of life. Few things will ever compare to that great calling. Those who have already served know what I mean. People saying "yes" for the first time will soon understand.

This book will never be on the *New York Times* bestseller list. That is reserved for titles like *The Art of the Deal*, *How to Get Rich*, and *Winning in Business*. There is no promise of fame or instructions on how to move with the power brokers in today's society. The people who embrace the principles presented here will not have economic, political, or military clout. They probably will not even gain more standing with the religious power base. But there will be incredible Kingdom moments for those who say "yes" to its principles and experiences of spiritual power that will last throughout all eternity. Few roles in life can offer so great an opportunity.

Other Books by the Author

Exalt Him: Designing Dynamic Worship Services (Christian Publications Inc.).

One to One: A Practical Guide to Friendship Evangelism (Christian Publishers Inc.).

Wounded: How to Find Inner Healing and Wholeness Through Him (Christian Publishers Inc.).

Draw Close to the Fire: Finding God in the Darkness (Leafwood Publishers).

Whispers of Love in Seasons of Fear (Chosen Books).

Healing Prayer, Healing Care: Helping the Broken Find Wholeness in Christ (Leafwood Publishers).

The Transforming Path: A Christ-Centered Approach to Spiritual Formation (Leafwood Publishers).

Outrageous Love, Transforming Power: How the Holy Spirit Shapes You into the Likeness of Christ (Sovereign World Publishers).

If you have enjoyed this book and would like to help us to
send a copy of it and many other titles to needy pastors in
the **Third World**, please write for further information
or send your gift to:

**Sovereign World Trust
PO Box 777, Tonbridge
Kent TN11 0ZS
United Kingdom**

or to the **'Sovereign World'** distributor in your country.

Visit our website at **www.sovereign-world.org**
for a full range of Sovereign World books.